Lady Gregory

THE IRISH WRITERS SERIES
James F. Carens, General Editor

TITLE	*AUTHOR*
SEAN O'CASEY	Bernard Benstock
J. C. MANGAN	James Kilroy
W. R. RODGERS	Darcy O'Brien
STANDISH O'GRADY	Phillip L. Marcus
PAUL VINCENT CARROLL	Paul A. Doyle
SEUMAS O'KELLY	George Brandon Saul
SHERIDAN LEFANU	Michael Begnal
AUSTIN CLARKE	John Jordan
BRIAN FRIEL	D. E. S. Maxwell
DANIEL CORKERY	George Brandon Saul
EIMAR O'DUFFY	Robert Hogan
MERVYN WALL	Robert Hogan
FRANK O'CONNOR	James Matthews
JAMES JOYCE	Fritz Senn
JOHN BUTLER YEATS	Douglas Archibald
LORD EDWARD DUNSANY	Zack Bowen
MARIA EDGEWORTH	James Newcomer
MARY LAVIN	Zack Bowen
OSCAR WILDE	Edward Partridge
SOMERVILLE AND ROSS	John Cronin
SUSAN L. MITCHELL	Richard M. Kain
J. M. SYNGE	Robin Skelton
KATHARINE TYNAN	Marilyn Gaddis Rose
LIAM O'FLAHERTY	James O'Brien
IRIS MURDOCH	Donna Gerstenberger
JAMES STEPHENS	Brigit Bramsback
BENEDICT KIELY	Daniel Casey
EDWARD MARTYN	Robert Christopher
DOUGLAS HYDE	Gareth Dunleavy
EDNA O'BRIEN	Grace Eckley
CHARLES LEVER	M. E. Elliott
BRIAN MOORE	Jeanne Flood
SAMUEL BECKETT	Clive Hart
ELIZABETH BOWEN	Edwin J. Kenney
JOHN MONTAGUE	Frank Kersnowski
ROBERT MATURIN	Robert E. Lougy
GEORGE FITZMAURICE	Arthur E. McGuinness
MICHAEL MCCLAVERTY	Leo F. McNamara

FRANCIS STUART	J. H. Natterstad
PATRICK KAVANAGH	Darcy O'Brien
BRINSLEY MACNAMARA AND GEORGE SHIELS	Raymond J. Porter
STEPHEN MACKENNA	Roger Rosenblatt
JACK B. YEATS	Robin Skelton
WILLIAM ALLINGHAM	Alan Warner
SAMUEL LOVER	Mabel Worthington
FLANN O'BRIEN	Bernard Benstock
DENIS JOHNSTON	James F. Carens
WILLIAM LARMINIE	Richard J. Finneran
SIR SAMUEL FERGUSON	Malcolm Brown
LADY GREGORY	Hazard Adams
GEORGE RUSSELL (AE)	Richard M. Kain and James O'Brien
DION BOUCICAULT	Peter A. Tasch
THOMAS DAVIS	Eileen Ibarra
LOUIS MACNEICE	Christopher Armitage
PADRAIC COLUM	Charles Burgess

LADY GREGORY

Hazard Adams

Lewisburg
BUCKNELL UNIVERSITY PRESS

Associated University Presses, Inc.
Cranbury, New Jersey 08512

REF
PR
4728
.G5
Z548

cap. 1

Library of Congress Cataloging in Publication Data
Adams, Hazard, 1926–
    Lady Gregory.

    (The Irish writers series)
    Bibliography: p.
    1. Gregory, Isabella Augusta (Persse) Lady, 1852–1932.
PR4728.G5Z548   822′.9′12   72-3253
ISBN 0-8387-1085-9
ISBN 0-8387-1207-X (pbk)

PRINTED IN THE UNITED STATES OF AMERICA

Contents

Preface

This short book contains an introductory chapter on Lady Gregory's life and career as a writer and concentrates thereafter on her dramatic writings and syncretic translations of Irish heroic legends. I assume that the reader can learn more than is mentioned here of her important role with the Abbey Theatre by consulting her own *Our Irish Theatre* and the several available books on the Irish dramatic movement.

Lady Gregory did not promote herself as a playwright. She tells us that as a young woman "living a good deal in London," she had never cared much for the stage, and she asserts modestly that she began to write her comedies in order to give the ear and mind of Abbey patrons a change of pace from the dominant poetic drama of W. B. Yeats. She insists that verse, in which she did not write after her first play, *Colman and Guaire* (never produced), is, "more than any prose can be, the apex of the flame, the point of the diamond." Her plays, especially the short curtain-lifting comedies, were extremely popular, and most were replayed with considerable success. Except for a few sympathetic studies, however, they have received scant critical attention and are seldom now seen at the Abbey. The role she chose to play has, no doubt, obscured her work.

Una Ellis-Fermor ends her chapter of *The Irish Dramatic Movement* on Lady Gregory as follows: ". . . her contribution to the movement was, even as a writer, still characteristically feminine; it provided the means or the medium by which men of genius could realize themselves." The two most recent studies, both by women, rise to the defense. Miss Elizabeth Coxhead, in her *Lady Gregory: A Literary Portrait,* criticizes Yeats's *Autobiography* for ignoring Lady Gregory's plays and the extent of Lady Gregory's hand in their collaborations. Miss Ann Saddlemyer entitles her short critical book *In Defence of Lady Gregory, Playwright.* These writers would rescue Lady Gregory's dramatic art from what seems to them critical oblivion, or at least the shadows of Yeats and Synge. It was a worthy aim, no doubt overdue. I follow upon them, in their debt, and in the debt of Una Ellis-Fermor and Lennox Robinson, hoping to describe and assess, as space will allow, Lady Gregory's achievement in her writings as a whole.

Acknowledgments

I wish to express my thanks particularly to Miss Elizabeth Coxhead for her permission to reprint Ruth Shine's photograph of Lady Gregory, which is in her possession, and to Mrs. Mary Gazlay, who typed and edited my manuscript.

The following acknowledgments are made for quotations in the text:

"To a Friend Whose Work Has Come To Nothing," copyright 1916 by The Macmillan Co., renewed 1944 by Bertha Georgie Yeats. Reprinted by permission.

"Beautiful Lofty Things," reprinted by permission of The Macmillan Co. from *Collected Poems* by W. B. Yeats. Copyright 1940 by Georgie Yeats, renewed 1968 by Bertha Georgie Yeats, Michael Butler Yeats and Anne Yeats.

Excerpts from the *Autobiography,* reprinted with permission of The Macmillan Co. from *The Autobiography of William Butler Yeats,* copyright 1916, 1936 by The Macmillan Co., renewed 1944 by Bertha Georgie Yeats.

Part of my discussion of *The Travelling Man* I have appropriated, revised, from my "Yeats's 'Country of the Young,'" *PMLA* 72, no. 3 (June 1957) : 510–19.

Finally, acknowledgment is made to Colin Smythe Ltd., Gerrards Cross, Bucks., England, publishers of The Coole Edition of Lady Gregory's works, for permission to quote the extracts of her writings in this book. The Coole Edition is published in the U.S.A. and Canada by the Oxford University Press, New York. Performing rights to the works of Lady Gregory are held by Samuel French, Inc.

Chronology

1852 (15 March)	Born at Roxborough House, Co. Galway
1879	Visit to Nice and Rome with her mother and invalid brother, Richard. Meets Sir William Gregory.
1880 (2 March)	Marriage to Sir William Gregory (age 63) in Dublin.
1881 (May)	Birth of their only child, Robert.
1881–82	Winter in Egypt.
ca. 1884	Writes unpublished manuscript, *An Emigrant's Notebook*.
ca. 1894	Begins to learn Irish.
1897	First talk of a theater with W. B. Yeats.
1899 (8 and 9 May)	First performances of the Irish Literary Theatre: Yeats's *The Countess Cathleen* and Edward Martyn's *The Heather Field*.
1901	*Colman and Guaire* written, never produced.
1902	*The Jackdaw* (revised 1907) and *A Losing Game* (revised 1903) written.

1902 (2 April)	*Cathleen ni Houlihan* (with Yeats) produced.
1902 (30 October)	*The Pot of Broth* (with Yeats) produced.
1903 (14 March)	First production of one of her plays, *Twenty-Five.*
1904 (27 December)	First performance of the Abbey Theatre: Yeats's *On Baile's Strand* and her *Spreading the News.*
1905 (25 March)	*Kincora* produced (later revised).
1905 (9 December)	*The White Cockade* produced.
1906 (19 February)	*Hyacinth Halvey* produced.
1906 (16 April)	*The Doctor in Spite of Himself* (Molière) produced.
1906 (20 October)	*The Gaol Gate* produced.
1906 (8 December)	*The Canavans* produced.
1907 (26 January)	Troubles at the Abbey over J. M. Synge's *The Playboy of the Western World.*
1907 (9 March)	*The Rising of the Moon* produced.
1907 (3 April)	*The Poorhouse* (with Douglas Hyde) produced.
1907 (31 October)	*Dervorgilla* produced.
1907 (21 November)	*The Unicorn from the Stars* (with W. B. Yeats) produced.
1908 (19 March)	*Teja* (Sudermann) produced.

1908 (4 April)	*The Rogueries of Scapin* (Molière) produced.
1908 (20 April)	*The Workhouse Ward* produced.
1909 (21 January)	*The Miser* (Molière) produced.
1909 (24 March)	Death of J. M. Synge.
1909 (August)	Troubles with Dublin Castle over G. B. Shaw's *The Showing Up of Blanco Posnet.*
1909 (11 November)	*The Image* produced.
1910 (24 February)	*Mirandolina* (Goldoni) produced.
1910 (2 March)	*The Travelling Man* produced.
1910 (10 November)	*The Full Moon* produced.
1910 (1 December)	*Coats* produced.
1911 (12 January)	*The Deliverer* produced.
ca. 1911	*Grania* written, never produced.
1911–1912 (September-March)	First American tour of the Abbey Players under her supervision.
1912 (11 January)	*MacDonough's Wife* produced.
1912 (4 July)	*The Bogie Men* produced.
1912 (21 November)	*Damer's Gold* produced.
1913	Second American tour.

1914	Third American tour.
1914	*The Wrens* produced.
(1 June)	
1915	*Shanwalla* produced.
(8 April)	
1915	Death of her nephew Sir Hugh Lane
(7 May)	on the *Lusitania*.
1918	*The Jester* written, not produced.
1918	Her son, Robert, shot down and
(23 January)	killed in Italy.
1918	*Hanrahan's Oath* produced.
(29 January)	
1919	She acts the lead in *Cathleen ni Houli-*
(18 March)	*han*.
1919	*The Dragon* produced.
(21 April)	
1920–1922	The Civil War. Coole in danger. Rox-borough burned.
1920–1921	She publishes anonymously a series
(October-	of essays on the troubles in the En-
January)	glish periodical *The Nation*.
1921	*Aristotle's Bellows* produced.
(17 March)	
1923	First play by Sean O'Casey at the
(12 April)	Abbey: *The Shadow of a Gunman*.
1923	Death of Edward Martyn.
(5 December)	
1923	"An Old Woman Remembers" re-
(31 December)	cited.
1926	*The Would-Be Gentleman* (Molière)
(4 January)	produced.
1926	She undergoes operation for cancer.
(September)	

1927 (14 March)	*Sancho's Master* (Cervantes) produced.
1927 (9 May)	*Dave* produced.
1927 (20 October)	Sale of Coole to the Department of Lands and Agriculture, subsequently rented by her until her death.
1928	The Abbey Theatre rejects O'Casey's *The Silver Tassie*. A dispute follows.
1932 (22 May)	She dies at Coole.

Lady Gregory was buried in Galway. Coole House, after standing for several years, was demolished.

Lady Gregory

1
Her Career

Isabella Augusta Persse was born into an Anglo-Irish, Protestant Ascendancy family at Roxborough House, County Galway, on March 15, 1852. She was the youngest daughter of Dudley Persse, who fathered sixteen children by two wives. She outlived them all and Roxborough, too, for the great house was occupied during the troubles of 1922 by the Irish Republican Army and subsequently burned. She met her husband-to-be, Sir William Gregory, on a visit to Italy in 1879 with her mother and an ailing brother. They were married in 1880. He was the owner of a country house and estate named Coole, only a few miles from Roxborough, a widower, sixty-three years old, and childless. She was twenty-eight. In May of 1881 their son, Robert, subject of Yeats's famous elegies, was born. Sir William died in 1892, and Augusta, Lady Gregory, never remarried.

Sir William Gregory was a man who just missed notoriety, for he nearly fought the last duel known in England. He did gain a measure of fame, nevertheless, for his government service. Sir William was descended from a landed Warwickshire family that had come into Ireland with Cromwell. His great-grandfather, Robert, made a fortune in the East India Company, twice served in parliament, then retired to Galway to build Coole Park, which, up until Sir William sold large portions in 1853 to pay racing debts, was a lucrative property. The grandfather, William, sat in the Irish Parliament in 1798–1800, served as high sheriff of Galway in 1799, and was civil undersecretary to the lord-lieutenant of Ireland from 1812 to 1831 as well as military undersecretary from 1821. Sir William's father, Robert, was apparently a quiet man, content to live his life at Coole, managing the estate and adding to its considerable library, or to travel abroad.

Lady Gregory's husband-to-be was a brilliant scholar at Harrow, attended Oxford, but left without taking a degree, won election to parliament for Dublin at age twenty-five, gaining the esteem of such politically divergent men as Peel, Disraeli, and O'Connell. Originally Tory, his politics were more often liberal, and he finally joined the Liberal Party in 1865, supported Catholic emancipation, and worked to improve the conditions of the Irish tenant farmer. After two periods of service in Parliament, 1842–1847 and 1857–1871, he was appointed governor of Ceylon and served for five years, spending "more money on reproductive works than any other governor, doing much to stimulate the cultivation of coffee and tea, and to improve the harbours of the island." He resigned what had been a most successful governorship, perhaps out of boredom, and returned to Ireland in 1877. In 1867 he had been appointed a trustee of the National Gallery, a position that he took very seriously, performing many important services. The *Dictionary of National*

Biography remarks that he was regarded as parliamentary expert on matters of art. The *Dictionary* also observes: "Gregory was a man of great natural abilities, real political talent, and marked personal charm, who, but for a certain inherent instability, might easily have attained to the most eminent political positions." His *Autobiography*, edited by Lady Gregory in 1894, reveals a forthright, honest, and unpretentious character.

Some of Augusta Persse's own liberal attitudes must have been encouraged and some developed as a result of marriage with this man. On the other hand, she was of strong will and imagination, and had developed as a child a deep attachment to her surroundings. These would early contribute to nationalistic and liberal sympathies:

> a romantic love of country had awakened in me, perhaps through the wide beauty of my home, from whose hillsides I could see the mountain of Burren and Iar Connacht, and at sunset the silver western sea; or it may be through the half revealed sympathy of my old nurse for the rebels whose cheering she remembered when the French landed at Killala in '98; or perhaps but through the natural breaking of a younger child of the house from the conservatism of her elders.

Also, the house to which she came when she married played a part. Coole had a distinguished history, a fine library. Lennox Robinson, recalling a comment by W. B. Yeats, remarks that if Balzac had written of the Gregorys he would have expended fifty pages describing the crowded walls, the library, and the pictures. Coole remained all of her life a principal joy and in later years a great worry, for it could not be sustained on her income and had finally to be sold to and rented back from the government. Her sentiment for it is frequently expressed in her journals:

> *February 22, 1924.* Last night in the Library the firelight, the lamplight, shining on the rich bindings of that wall of books, and this evening, by the lake, so silent and beautiful, Crannagh so peaceful—"the tilled, familiar land"; and later as I went upstairs and looked from my window at the sunset behind the blue range of hills I felt so grateful, as I have often done of late, to my husband who brought me to this house and home.

The house has been immortalized in several of Yeats's poems, and Lady Gregory herself published a small book about it in 1931.

By the time of Sir William's death in 1892, Augusta Gregory's literary career gave little indication of the flight it would take after her momentous meetings with Yeats in 1897 and 1898. She had published in 1882 the pamphlet *Arabi and His Household* as a result of time spent with her husband in Egypt and of her interest in the anti-Turkish Egyptian officer Arabi Pasha, who was receiving a bad press in London, for he was a symbol of nationalist feeling. The pamphlet is characteristic of Lady Grgeory's approach—the same that made her such an effective recorder of folk tales among the Connacht peasantry. She tries to describe the man and his real life among his people and possessions, and thus to discredit false, exaggerated stories about him.

In about 1884 she wrote an unpublished manuscript entitled *An Emigrant's Notebook.* It is, as Elizabeth Coxhead has remarked, "a series of agreeable anecdotes strung together." But she quite rightly adds that it does show that her literary personality was in the process of formation before she met Yeats and Douglas Hyde.

It is concerned with events at Roxborough during the
Land League agitation, and the characters are those of
servants on the estate. In this work there appears the
nurse Mary Sheridan, who sharpened the child Augusta's interest in fairy and folk tales with an apparently
limitless hoard of such lore.

Lady Gregory's other early work is limited to editing
her husband's autobiography and letters written to
and from his grandfather during his political career.
Interesting as these works may be for a number of
reasons, they are no more than might be expected of
the widow of a fairly well-known public servant from
an Ascendancy family.

It was, of course, not merely her meeting with Yeats
that made a writer of her, though it was certainly the
main catalytic experience. Indeed, from her youth under the tutelage of Mary Sheridan she had developed
an interest in what we may roughly call mythology. It
was to provide her the basis for everything she was
later to write, whether it was to be the syncretic retelling of early Irish legends, the creation of her own
mythical town of Cloon, or the composition of wonder
plays. Her inventiveness went beyond Yeats's remark
about her in his autobiography:

> During these first years Lady Gregory was friend and
> hostess, a centre of peace, an adviser who never overesti-
> mated or underestimated trouble, but neither she nor
> we thought her a possible creator. And now all in a
> moment, as it seemed, she became the founder of modern
> Irish dialect literature.

It only seemed that her talent miraculously developed,
and her contribution was far greater than Yeats claimed

for her here. He also asserts that her *Cuchulain of Muirthemne* and *Gods and Fighting Men* were

> made possible by her past; semi-feudal Roxborough, her inherited sense of caste, her knowledge of that top of the world where men and women are valued for their manhood and their charm, not for their opinions, her long study of Scottish Ballads, of Percy's *Reliques,* of the *Morte d'Arthur.* If she had not found those tales, or finding them had not found the dialect of Kiltartan, that past could not, as it were, have drawn itself together, come to birth as present personality.

—A Yeatsian judgment, displaying his own biases, but true enough as far as it goes.

Yeats mentions in passing that those who did not know Lady Gregory thought her stern. Perhaps this is a hint at the existence of a power within her that made her a woman of action and of authority. It was a matter not simply of her background but of her clash with and assimilation of it. Yeats writes,

> She knew Ireland always in its permanent relationships, associations,—violence but a brief interruption—never lost her sense of feudal responsibility, not of duty as the word is generally understood, but of burdens laid upon her by her station and her character, a choice constantly renewed in solitude.

One senses that she was a private personality with immense capacity for work.

After her husband's death she retreated into widow's weeds for life, though she was only forty. A remark by Seaghan Barlow reported by Lennox Robinson is revealing: "Lady Gregory never forgot to show appreciation of any effort, even when it was not successful.

In fact, she was, at times, so lavish in praise that one was inclined to suspect her sincerity." A certain reticence, even perhaps a slight uneasiness with others of another class, may reveal itself here. Sean O'Casey once wrote to her:

> You can always walk with your head up. And remember you had to fight against your birth into position and comfort, as others had to fight against their birth into hardship and poverty, and it is as difficult to come out of one as it is to come out of the other, so that power may be gained to bring fountains and waters out of the hard rocks.

This is oversimplification, I suspect, but there is a point to it.

In her last years, as her journals show, the admirable quality of fighting persistence, of which nearly everyone who knew her remarked, appears a bit pathetic in her dogged battles to save Coole from destruction and to influence England to return the art collections of her nephew Hugh Lane to Dublin. Had she been successful in these efforts, and reasonably quickly, we would think nothing of them except to observe that effort and result were in character. In prolonged frustration, a weakened old woman, she reveals a tenacity slightly embarrassing, almost of rote habit. She said of herself: "I have myself a leaning toward sentimentality." That tendency is perhaps not out of keeping with other characteristics that preserved her isolation from all but a rather small circle of friends. Her outward emotions themselves, like her plays, were apparently highly disciplined and subject to her own moral imperatives. Late in life, a journal entry for January 1, 1928, says: "Love, the solution of life, of living in heaven while on earth. I seem to grasp it sometimes; it would set everything right if I could feel to all as I do to, say, Richard [her grandchild]." Yet Yeats remembers an old peasant who said to him, "She has been like a serving-maid among us. She is plain and simple, like the Mother of God, and that was the greatest lady that ever lived."

She was, then, vigorous, austere, but capable of reaching beyond the confines of her own class and her own kind. She was also witty, but accounts of her rarely reveal this. Her comedies do. Wit is suppressed even in her journals, which contain a great deal of sentiment, particularly in connection with Coole. She was treated with respect and in some quarters not a little fear. Lennox Robinson, who had his occasional differences with her, writes: "With much of the Spartan in her, she demanded the same qualities from others. On the day that her son was born, her husband and she were entertaining some distinguished guests at luncheon. After lunch she went upstairs and had her baby—and probably came down in time to pour out tea." He calls her "a fine fighter" and always for principle. And in Yeats's poem "Beautiful Lofty Things," there are these lines:

Augusta Gregory seated at her great ormolu table,
Her eightieth winter approaching: "Yesterday he
        threatened my life.
I told him that nightly from six to seven I sat at this table,
The blinds drawn up."

One can probably attribute some of the making of her artistic consciousness to Mary Sheridan and her store of folklore. The rest that is not mysteriously internal to her individuality we must attribute to the confluence of place, time, and friends. Place, of course, gave her the Kiltartan dialect in which she wrote nearly all of her works. It was around her in her childhood, and she kept her connections with it through her local marriage and her continued residence at Coole. As her own interest in myth grew, contemporary efforts to revive the Irish language as part of the nationalistic movement supported it. From early youth, though of Ascendancy upbringing, Augusta Persse had nationalistic sympathies. In *Our Irish Theatre* she quotes herself in conversation with a gentleman who had remarked to her, "I see a tendency to Home Rule on your own part." Her reply: "I defy anyone to study Irish history without getting a dislike and distrust of England." She came to know the leader of the Irish revival, Douglas Hyde, founder and president of the Gaelic League and later president of Ireland. His interest was to reestablish spoken Irish, and he became himself a poet and playwright in that language. Of Hyde's founding the Gaelic League she wrote in *The Kiltartan Poetry Book:*

> through it country people were gathered together in the Irish speaking places to give the songs and poems, old and new, kept in their memory. This discovery, this disclosure of the folk learning, the folk poetry, the ancient tradition, was the small beginning of a weighty change. It was an upsetting of the table of values, an astonishing excitement. The imagination of Ireland had found a new homing place. My own imagination was aroused. I was becoming conscious of a world close to me and that I had been ignorant of. It was not now in the corners of newspapers I looked for poetic emotion, nor even to the singers in the streets. It was among farmers and potato diggers and old men in workhouses and beggars at my own door.

In his poems Hyde consciously wrote to catch traditional phrase and rhythm. His translations in *Love*

Songs of Connacht (1893) brought to her the realiza-
tion that "the people about me had been keeping up
the lyrical tradition that existed in Ireland before
Chaucer lived." *Poets and Dreamers* (1903) includes
an essay on Hyde's poems and translations into English
of four of Hyde's plays including the well-known
Cusadh an Sughain (*The Twisting of the Rope*), the
first play in Irish ever given in Dublin. In her book
she attributes the beginning of modern drama in Irish
to Hyde's acting in a Punch and Judy show in 1898
in Coole. Her appreciation of Hyde's work passes over
his nationalistic ballads to concentrate on the "more
personal poems." She thinks, however, that his own
love poems do not equal those of his translations, which
she had read several years before she met him. Hyde's
best-known plays were really collaborations with Lady
Gregory, occasionally with Yeats's help:

> he wrote *The Twisting of the Rope,* based on one of
> Mr. Yeats's Hanrahan stories; *The Lost Saint* on a legend
> given its shape by Mr. Yeats, and *The Nativity* on a
> scenario we wrote together for him. Afterwards he wrote
> *The Marriage* and *The Poorhouse,* upon in each case a
> scenario written by me. I betray no secret in telling this,
> for Dr. Hyde has made none of the collaboration, giving
> perhaps too generous acknowledgment.

Hyde never developed as a poet, and his contribution
to the movement was largely through his work on
behalf of the language. Lady Gregory's friendship with
him was an encouragement for her own interests. She
observed of him in *Our Irish Theatre* that his founding
of the Gaelic League was of immense importance to
their work:

It was a movement for keeping the Irish language a
spoken one, with, as a chief end, preserving of our own
nationality. That does not sound like the beginning of
a revolution, yet it was one. It was the discovery, the
disclosure of the folk-learning, the folk-poetry, the folk-
tradition. Our Theatre was caught into that current, and
it is that current, as I believe, that has brought it on its
triumphant way.

Her meeting with Yeats was decisive for her because
it turned her interests in the direction of the theater,
gave her friendship with literary genius, and further
encouraged her interest in myth and folklore. She had
been acquainted with Yeats's early *Fairy and Folk Tales
of the Irish Peasantry* (1888) and his poems and stories
in the same vein, so knew of his interests, and they
were sympathetic with each other from the outset. Lady
Gregory recalls the visit of the poet:

On one of those days at Duras [summer home of her
friend the Count de Basterot], in 1898 [it is thought that
she errs and that the meeting took place in 1897], Mr.
Edward Martyn, my neighbor, came to see the Count,
bringing with him Mr. Yeats, whom I did not then know
very well, though I cared for his work very much and
had already, through his directions, been gathering folklore. . . . Though I had never been at all interested in
theatres, our talk turned on plays. Mr. Martyn had written two, *The Heather Field* and *Maeve*. . . . I said it was
a pity we had no Irish theatre where such plays could
be given. Mr. Yeats said that it had always been a dream
of his, but he had of late thought it an impossible one,
for it could not at first pay its way, and there was no
money to be found for such a thing in Ireland.

We went on talking about it, and things seemed to
grow possible as we talked, and before the end of the
afternoon we had made our plan.

According to Ann Saddlemyer it was Lady Gregory's nationalism that took her to the theater. But I venture to say that it was also a combination of her literary and folk interests, the friendship with Yeats, and her own immense energy that set her on course. The proposal by which they were to attract guarantors she later thought a trifle pompous. It was doubtless Yeats's for the most part, but she subscribed to it:

> We propose to have performed in Dublin, in the spring of every year certain Celtic and Irish plays, which whatever be their degree of excellence will be written with a high ambition, and so to build up a Celtic and Irish school of dramatic literature. We hope to find in Ireland an uncorrupted and imaginative audience trained to listen by its passion for oratory. . . .

Lady Gregory herself claimed not to have understood the mention of Celtic: "I used to say it was a movement meant to persuade the Scotch to begin buying our books, while we continued not to buy theirs."

The history of the Irish dramatic movement is told in a number of places. It must suffice to recount the following: The "Irish Literary Theatre" gave its first performances May 8 and 9, 1899, with Yeats's *Countess Cathleen* and Martyn's *Heather Field*. After various offerings under different organizational names, the Abbey Theatre was founded on December 27, 1904, with Lady Gregory's *Spreading the News* and Yeats's *Hour Glass* performed. It was her second performed play, the first, *Twenty-Five,* having been offered by the Irish National Theatre Society a year before. She was then fifty years old.

As it turned out, although Miss A. E. F. Horniman, an Englishwoman, put up the money for the theater and a modest subsidy, Lady Gregory was the patentee and, after enquiry, was "enjoined and commanded to gather, entertain, govern, privilege, and keep such and so many players" and not to allow on the stage "exhibition of wild beasts or dangerous performances or to allow women or children to be hung from the flies or fixed in positions from which they cannot release themselves."

As one of the three directors of the Abbey—the other two were Yeats and Synge—Lady Gregory endorsed and helped to formulate its policies. She was as committed as Yeats to serious artistic purpose. She remarks in her account of their early years that they were often advised to become more popular and offer "work that would draw an audience for the moment from being topical, or because the author had friends in some league. But we went on giving what we thought good until it became popular." Her aim, and Yeats's, was not to humor the audience but to "educate" it. Yet they abhorred indoctrination and propaganda. Yeats's advice to playwrights, printed and sent out with rejected manuscripts, reflected her views as well as his:

> The Abbey Theatre is a subsidised theatre with an educational object. It will, therefore, be useless as a rule to send it plays intended as popular entertainments and that alone, or originally written for performance by some popular actor at the popular theatres. A play to be suitable for performance at the Abbey should contain some criticism of life, founded on the experience or personal observation of the writer, or some vision of life, of Irish life by preference, important from its beauty or from some excellence of style; and this intellectual quality is not more necessary to tragedy than to the gayest comedy.
> We do not desire propagandist plays, nor plays written mainly to serve some obvious moral purpose; for art

seldom concerns itself with those interests or opinions that can be defended by argument, but with realities of emotion and character that become self-evident when made vivid to the imagination.

The dramatist should also banish from his mind the thought that there are some ingredients, the love-making of the popular stage for instance, especially fitted to give dramatic pleasure; for any knot of events, where there is passionate emotion and clash of will, can be made the subject matter of a play. . . . Young writers should remember that they must get all their effects from the logical expression of their subject, and not by the addition of extraneous incidents. . . . A work of art, though it must have the effect of nature, is art because it is not nature, as Goethe said: and it must possess a unity unlike the accidental profusion of nature.

The Abbey Theatre is continually sent plays which show that their writers have not understood that the attainment of this unity by what is usually a long shaping and reshaping of the plot, is the principal labour of the dramatist, and not the writing of the dialogue.

How fully Lady Gregory subscribed to these views, particularly the strictures on the importance of shaping the plot, can be seen by a study of her own dramas, which are so often models of the well-made play. It must have given her great pleasure to read in *The Irish Peasant* a review of her *Hyacinth Halvey* in which play and production were recognized to have achieved the desired ends: ". . . nothing is ever overdone, there is never the least appeal to the gallery; the faults are never of the fixed kind that limit progress, and there is never an attempt to magnify a part at the expense of the artistic symmetry of the whole."

In matters that concerned the principles upon which the Abbey was founded, she was unbending, as the times required, and she subjected her own judgments to criticism. In a letter she complained:

We have been humouring our audience instead of educating it, which is the work we ought to do. . . . I only read Gerothwohl's speech after you left, and thought that sentence most excellent about the theatre he was connected with being intended "for art and a thinking Democracy." It is just what we set out to do, and now we are giving in to stupidity in a Democracy.

They should have two horizons, she told Lennox Robinson in 1919: ". . . the far one, the laying of it [the Abbey Theatre] 'on the threshold of Eternity'; the nearer one the coming of Home Rule. . . . We must keep the Theatre something we should be proud to show." At seventy-five, as her journal shows, she was not ready to tolerate any less:

I did feel proud and satisfied—a Theatre of our own, Irish plays, such a fine one by our countryman [Shaw]— company playing it so splendidly, all our own—something to have lived to see! But there is a good deal of slackness at the Abbey.

By that time she had fought many battles, beginning with the riots over Synge's *Playboy of the Western World* in Dublin in 1907, and subsequent troubles when she took the company to America in 1911. In passing, it may be remarked that she herself did not care for *The Playboy*. She also had engaged in a prolonged struggle with Dublin Castle over the right to perform Shaw's *The Showing Up of Blanco Posnet,* all this being recounted simply and directly in *Our Irish Theatre*. The Abbey triumphed over these problems and in so doing kept faith with its principles, for attention gradually turned from demands for the trite and superficial demagogic nationalism of a sentimental and provincial theater to acceptance of a far deeper, critical love.

Her friendship with Yeats, of course, did much to stimulate her already abundant interest in folklore. When Yeats came to visit at Coole, exhausted by his frustrating love affair with Maud Gonne and in bad health, Lady Gregory engaged his interest by taking him out hunting folk tales:

> [She] brought me from cottage to cottage collecting folk-lore. Every night she wrote out what we had heard in the dialect of the cottages. She wrote, if memory does not deceive me, two hundred thousand words, discovering that vivid English she was the first to use upon the stage.

Yeats was searching for "actual experience of the supernatural"; it was really Lady Gregory who was the scholarly folklorist. This is reflected in the books that grew from her research, and perhaps most succinctly in the essay on the blind poet Raftery in her *Poets and Dreamers*. Raftery, who lived from about 1780 to about 1840, was rediscovered by Douglas Hyde through conversations and by running across a manuscript of some of his poems in the Royal Irish Academy. He was a destitute, wandering bard and fiddler. He had never been taught to read or write, yet he seems to have exerted a tremendous influence on those who knew him during his tramps through Mayo and Galway. Lady Gregory was obviously fascinated by him, giving an account of his poetic "contentions" with the farmer poet Callinan and arguing that he represented the old bardic tradition of over 2,000 years' duration. It was she who finally located his grave in Killeenan and erected a marker over it. A figure rather like Raftery, who seems to have meant so much to her, appears in one of her finest plays, *MacDonough's Wife* (1912). MacDonough is drawn from a local piper who had played at festivities when she moved to Coole and later at her son's coming of age. The one act of which the play is composed is without complexity of plot. It tells of the return of MacDonough to his home in Galway to find his wife dead and no one willing to keen her loss or to bury her except two hags, for the people have never accepted her. The play rises through Mac-Donough's despair and self-castigation to his decision to play his pipes in lament for her, drawing people from their doors to follow her coffin through the streets. This act is also an assertion of his own dignity as an artist: ". . . I am of the generations of Orpheus, and have in me the breed of his master! And of Raftery and Carolan and O'Daly and all that made sounds of music from this back to the foundations of the earth!" He represents the traditions of the very people he must induce to come with him. He is, in a way, their dignity, the living symbol of an unwritten history, a message to them.

In addition to giving an account of Raftery and re-producing Hyde's plays in translation, *Poets and Dreamers* offers collections of Boer, West Irish, and Jacobite ballads. In *The Kiltartan Poetry Book* (1918), in which some of this material reappears, she describes the sources:

An Aran man, repeating to me *The Grief of a Girl's Heart* in Irish told me it was with that song his mother had often sung him to sleep as a child. It was from an old woman who had known Mary Hynes and who said of her, "the sun and the moon never shone upon anything so handsome" that I first heard Raftery's song of praise of her, "the pearl that was at Ballylee," a song "that has gone around the world & as far as America." It was in a stonecutter's house where I went to have a headstone made for Raftery's grave that I found a manuscript book of his poems, written out in the clear beautiful Irish characters. It was to a working farmer's house I walked on many a moonlit evening with the manuscript that his greater knowledge helped me to understand and by his hearth that I read for the first time the *Vision of Death* and the *Lament for O'Daly*. After that I met with many old people who had in the days before the Famine seen or talked with the wandering poet who was in the succession of those who had made and recited their lyrics on the Irish roads before Chaucer wrote.

She found versions of the older mythological cycles to be present among the folk. She heard tales of Cuchulain's fight with his son, of Deirdre, and of Grania from a man a century old and in many places "of Osgar's bravery and Goll's strength and Conan's bitter tongue, and the arguments of Oisin and Patrick." It was in these experiences that *Cuchulain of Muirthemne, Gods and Fighting Men,* and *Visions and Beliefs in the West of Ireland* began to take shape. Yeats had been approached to attempt a retelling of the heroic cycles, but could not give the time. When Lady Gregory volunteered, he could see "nothing in her past to fit her for that work," but as with her plays he was soon astonished. Asserting that "we work to add dignity to Ireland," she soon produced her first translation in the Kiltartan dialect. In *Our Irish Theatre* she took pride in recognizing that the Abbey "is chiefly known now as a folk-theatre. It has not only the great mass of primitive material and legend to draw on, but it has been made a living thing by the excitement of that discovery."

Ernest Boyd argued that the translations of Standish Hayes O'Grady were probably more influential than those of Lady Gregory. They did play a decisive role in reviving the old stories. Lady Gregory always acknowledged their influence upon her, but it was her works, written in her particular style, that made the tales attractively available, especially to the writers of her time.

She was the only one of the major Abbey playwrights who successfully learned Irish. (Synge knew only a little.) She became a scholar of the tongue when her son expressed a desire to learn it. There had been two previous efforts, one when she was a child at Roxborough, but fear of mockery tempered her request for a teacher, and it was ignored. Later, after she married, she enlisted the aid of a gardener on the estate, but he apparently suspected her of some devious mockery and was not conscientious. The efforts of the Gaelic League had not yet made the study fashionable. She recalls a visit by Hyde to Coole when some old neighbor ladies, hearing that one visitor "was a gentleman who spoke to the beaters in Irish," remarked that he could not possibly be a gentleman if he spoke that language.

Lady Gregory's later years were marked by personal tragedy and Ireland's violent political troubles. From the latter she tried to remain reasonably aloof—mainly, one supposes, for the sake of the Abbey Theatre and Coole. She had held political humanitarian views from an early age, and there is no doubt that she was a nationalist of not always suppressed emotions. Lennox Robinson writes:

> returning one night from the Abbey Theatre, the Theatre's secretary was conducting her to her tram. It was in the worst days of the Black-and-Tan regime. A lorry was ambushed, shots rang out, and the secretary begged her to lie down on the pavement. Her reply was "Never!" and she drew herself up to her full height—she was not a tall woman—and at the top of her small voice shouted

"Up the Rebels!" About the same time an acquaintance of mine was in a tram with her, some trouble started between Irish and English, the tram had to stop, she climbed on the seat, looking keenly out, clapping her hands, and singing under her breath some patriotic ballad.

Her own journals are full of accounts of Black-and-Tan outrages. In the Civil War her sympathies gradually became republican, in contrast to Yeats's, but "without malice." She had hoped for help from Michael Collins in the matter of Hugh Lane's pictures and was saddened by his death in a Republican ambush, and as she thought of the violent acts of bloodshed on both sides she could only remark, "And all for that wretched Oath." (The War had been set off by the refusal of the Republicans to take the oath of allegiance to the king in the Irish Free State parliament.) In 1923 she writes: "I told Father O'Kelly one should not be more angry with Government or Republicans than with different sections of one's own mind, tilting to good or bad on one or the other side, in many questions besides this."

All during the terror and the troubles Coole stood unharmed, mainly because of her reputation as a patriot. During the terror she contributed a series of articles to the English weekly, *The Nation,* anonymously for fear of reprisals against Coole by one of the combatant sides.

The deaths of her nephew Hugh Lane on the *Lusitania* in 1915 and her son, Robert, in the war in Italy in 1918 were severe blows. Hugh's death brought about the controversy with England over his collection of French Impressionist paintings. Shortly before his death he had written a codicil to his will, offering the

pictures to Dublin if the city could provide a suitable
gallery. Unfortunately, the codicil was not witnessed.
Lady Gregory spent great effort to secure the pictures
for Ireland and to arrange for a proper gallery. It was
over thirty years after her death, however, that the
Municipal Gallery obtained the pictures. She died
thinking she had failed to obtain them, after approaching almost everyone in authority on both sides of the
Irish Sea.

Robert Gregory was a talented designer and painter,
and Lady Gregory's only child. She did not learn that
his fighter plane had been shot down by mistake by
Allied forces. That irony, which is unknowingly under-
lined in Yeats's "An Irish Airman Foresees His Death,"
was mercifully kept from her. She survived the tragedy
and turned much of her attention to her grandchildren,
especially the young Richard, and to the preservation
of Coole for them. Here again she failed after many
efforts, and Coole eventually was sold to the government, though she resided there as a tenant until her
death. Then the old historic house was torn down and
much of the land was logged. Over her journals hovers
the spirit of an age that was passing, the lingering
melancholy of an old woman, now ill with cancer, presiding over a dying estate. On Richard Gregory's
twenty-first birthday in 1930 she wrote in her journal:

> it is a contrast to Robert's coming-of-age, with the gather-
> ing of cousins and the big feast and dance for the ten-
> ants—Coole no longer ours. But the days of landed prop-
> erty have passed. It is better so. Yet I wish some one of
> our blood would after my death care enough for what
> has been a home for so long, to keep it open.

Even here, near death, she could see the justice in

loss and the possibility of a better world, just as she had seen in her widowhood a kind of growth:

> If I had not married I should not have learned the quick enrichment of sentences that one gets in conversation; had I not been widowed I should not have found the detachment of mind, the leisure for observation necessary to give insight into character, to express and interpret it. Loneliness made me rich—"full" as Bacon says.

Lady Gregory has left surprisingly little commentary upon dramatic theory. Her journals, for example, are almost entirely devoid of artistic speculation. Indeed, what little she did write is rather simple. Una Ellis-Fermor has remarked that she was a playwright whose dramatic theory is "almost entirely practice . . . it would seem as if she never had a theory about how a thing should be done until she came to do it. Even a scenario that she had sketched briefly would change in her hands—to her delighted surprise." Generally, what theory she expressed seems to have been derived from pronouncements by Yeats as enunciated in his "The Tragic Theatre" (1910). In that essay he distinguishes between tragedy and comedy by observing that "character is continuously present in comedy alone," that in tragedy lyric feeling overwhelms character and explores it by "passions and motives." Lady Gregory's remarks on her *Damer's Gold* (published 1913) almost surely reflect in over-simplified form Yeats's pronouncements:

> tragedy shows humanity in the grip of circumstance, of fate, of what our people call "the thing will happen," "the Woman in the Stars that does all". . . . Well, you put your actor in the grip of this woman, in the claws of the cat. Once in that grip you know what the end must be. You may let your hero kick and struggle, but he is

in the claws all the time, it is a mere question as to how nearly you will let him escape, and when you will allow the pounce. Fate itself is the protagonist, your actor cannot carry much character, it is out of place. You do not want to know the character of a wrestler you see trying his strength at a show.

One may make some observations about this remark coming from Lady Gregory. First, it may apply obliquely to Yeats's tragedies, where there is a high degree of ritualized action and the characters seem to be symbolic creatures playing roles in a preordained cosmic dance; but it is difficult, as we shall see, to apply it to Lady Gregory's most ambitious tragedies—*Grania* and *Kincora*. Second, Lady Gregory's pronouncement sounds rather like that of someone who is primarily a writer of comedies and is equating character with the Renaissance conception of "humour." Indeed, in his essay Yeats seems to do the same, quoting Congreve on the idea of "humour," which is: ". . . a singular and unavoidable way of doing anything peculiar to one man only, by which his speech and actions are distinguished from all other men."

Lady Gregory is arguing in her note that because of the element of "fate" tragedy is easier to write than comedy—at least easier for her. She tells us that she had begun to write comedy because the Abbey needed such plays. Perhaps she is attempting to assert the dignity of her own tragedies, which did not have the popular success of her comedies. In any case, it is difficult to take her pronouncements very seriously. The tragedies, as we shall see, are often the study of character, and the situations are often more open than her idea of the fated tragic implies. Perhaps her pronouncements come from the fact that her plays by and large are of the "well-made" sort; they have carefully constructed plots that emphasize the movement of the action. Perhaps it is best to say that her plays seem Aristotelian, with the comic conventions of Molière in the background. Her emphasis, as Ann Saddlemyer has argued, is upon fable and construction rather than emotion. Her work, however, is a flight not from emotion but from sentimentality. Knowing something of her own nature, one is hardly surprised at this, nor at her respect for Molière, as in her note on *The Doctor in Spite of Himself,* where she admires his work for its "roughness and simplicity, as of some old humorous folk-tale."

When Lady Gregory is mentioned as a playwright, it is most often her invention of the Kiltartan dialect drama that is remarked, but her plays are also characterized by the genius of their construction, her capacities for mythmaking, and her power therein to universalize the existence of the corner of the world that she made her subject.

2
Mythological History

Writing of his youth, Yeats remarked that, nine-
teenth-century science having deprived him of "the
simple-minded religion of my childhood, I had made
a new religion, almost an infallible church of poetic
tradition, of a fardel of stories, and of personages, and
of emotions. . . ." The spirit of this remark can be
found hovering over the writings of numerous authors
of his time. It is expressed in critical debates over the
problem of belief, in laments over the disappearance
of common myths, such as those out of which Dante
wrote his *Commedia,* and in romantic internalizations
of quest motifs. Yeats's statement is personal; he sought
to deal with his problem by rediscovering poetic conventions in underground sources—astrology, theosophy,
and neo-Platonic symbolism. Lady Gregory's view of
her work was in this sense less romantic, less subjective,
and more self-consciously purposeful and public. She
was, like Yeats, a mythmaker, but her work grew more
directly and more consistently than did Yeats's out of
the local life she observed and the life she read about
in the Irish sagas.

Ireland had become a country nearly bereft of its language and its mythology. Leprechaun and wolfhound, the popular icons, were no more than the Mickey Mouse and Pluto of America: the symbols of national sentimentality. The intellectual and artistic side of the nationalistic movement had as its task to restore the language and the old tales. Otherwise, cultural models would continue to be those imposed from England, and the Irish would remain similar to the models for the women in Lady Gregory's *The Gaol Gate,* who described themselves as "astray and terrified 'like blind beasts in a bog.' " It has long been recognized that mythology is not purely historical. Indeed, mythology performs a social or cultural function that history cannot perform. History can be only a contrary to myth, not a corrective so much as a means of liberation from a mythology that has become too culturally restrictive and brutalizing. This is the perpetual problem in a sovereign nation, one would think. But Ireland was not free and had not been for centuries. Its traditional cultural forms had been suppressed systematically by massive political power. Ireland did not, then, require the contrariety of history and the emancipatory power of fact and science. Rather, it required a mythology, built out of the fundamental life of the people. Yeats's attacks on rationalism and scientism were also attacks on the English oppressor. His characterization of the Celt as emotionally contrary to the English is really the expression of an ideal image, a mythology that could effect a containment and civilizing of the rational powers. When Lady Gregory defended the Abbey Theatre against "patriotic" attacks, she was also defending the re-creation of an Irish mythology.

Giambattista Vico pointed out long ago that "poetic" knowledge, or mythology, identifies beginnings. Myth, in Mircea Eliade's sense, constructs a sacred history of the primordial reality of a culture with exemplary models. It provides a means by which these models are ritually reborn in the retelling, which is the traditional function of the poet. Not moral codes, mythologies express the social fabric from which codes are abstracted. By apprehending the myth, as Eliade remarks, one knows the "origin" of things, but not in the temporal sense or in an external or abstract way. One lives *in* a myth; one lives *by* a code.

The real Irish world, shaped by its ancient language and mythology, had been pushed farther and farther from the original "pale" around Dublin to the western regions of the island. Of course, it went underground too, persisting where it did in oral form. No play had been presented in Dublin in Irish until Hyde's *Cusadh an Sugain*. Irish was hardly studied at all until the language revival, and the mythological cycles were denigrated by the professors, whom Lady Gregory takes to task in her preface to *Cuchulain of Muirthemne* and in notes to her *Gods and Fighting Men*. Dr. Atkinson of Trinity College had testified before the Commission of Intermediate Education that the old literature of Ireland was isolated, "almost intolerably low in tone— I do not mean naughty, but low," and lacking in idealism and imagination.

There had been considerable scholarship in the nineteenth century on the saga material, including the work of the pioneer Eugene O'Curry (1796–1862), H. D'Arbois de Jubainville, Kuno Meyer, Whitley Stokes, and Alfred Nutt. Translators preceding Lady Gregory included Standish Hayes O'Grady, whose work

History of Ireland: Heroic Period (1878) and *History of Ireland: Cuchulain and his Contemporaries* (1880) Yeats said "started us all." Yet O'Grady's work was written in a flowery style of the time and did not catch any recognizably Irish mode of speech. After O'Grady, Lady Gregory was the popularizer of the movement, and she was the first to render Irish mythical history in an Irish idiom. Her *Cuchulain of Muirthemne* (1902) is dedicated to the people of Kiltartan in the style she adopted from them: "I have told the whole story in plain and simple words, in the same way my old nurse Mary Sheridan used to be telling stories from the Irish long ago, and I a child at Roxborough."

The principal Irish mythology is twofold. The one part, which is Lady Gregory's concern in *Gods and Fighting Men* (1904), tells of the coming of the Tuatha de Danaan (the people of the goddess Danu) to Ireland, their victories over their predecessors, the Firbolgs and the Fomorians, in two epochal battles, the second of which gained for them full supremacy over the land. It goes on to describe the ultimate defeat of the Tuatha by the Gaels and their subsequent disappearance underground, where they persisted, ghostlike, as those shadowy supernatural figures, the Sidhe (Shee). The coming of the Gaels ends the age of the gods and ushers in that of the heroes, the Fianna, or sons of the heroic figure, Finn, first among whom was Oisin (Usheen), also the last survivor. He returned from a long sojourn in the Country of the Young to find Ireland Christianized, and he lived on to engage in dialogues with St. Patrick.

The other cycle of tales is that of the Red Branch heroes of Ulster, centering on the reign of King Conchubar (Conachoor) and the heroic exploits of Cuchulain (Cuhoolin or Cuhullin). The most celebrated of these stories is the *Tain bo Cuailnge* (cattle raid of Cooley), in which Queen Maeve of Connacht attempts to kidnap a fabulous brown bull from Conchubar's domain, only to be frustrated by the valor of Cuchulain.

Lady Gregory's *Gods and Fighting Men* tells the principal stories of the Tuatha, Finn, and Oisin. Her *Cuchulain of Muirthemne* (Mur-hev-na) is a syncretic rendering of the tales of the Ulster heroes, taking the life of Cuchulain as the main thread. This device provides an organizational principle, emphasizes the exploits of an incredibly heroic and lone spirit, and yet does not prevent her from offering a few important interludes in which Cuchulain himself does not figure prominently. One of these is the story of Deirdre, from which Yeats and Synge made famous plays.

In his preface to *Cuchulain* Yeats emphasizes the lyric impulse of the Irish as against the narrative, factual interest of the Danes in order to explain the diffuseness of the story or stories Lady Gregory tells. Actually, though, Lady Gregory's arrangement has brought a considerable order into the mass of her sources. She has also sharpened and clarified the traditional characters and, as Yeats remarked, given to the women of the stories a special attractiveness:

Women indeed, with their lamentations for lovers and husbands and sons, and for fallen rooftrees and lost wealth, give the stories their most beautiful sentences; and, after Cuchulain, we think most of certain great queens—of angry, amorous Maeve, with her long pale face; of Findabair, her daughter, who dies of shame and of pity; of Deirdre who might be some mild modern housewife but for her prophetic wisdom.

Thomas Kinsella, who has recently translated the *Tain,* using not the *Book of Leinster* as his principal source but the earlier *Lebor na hUidre* (*Book of the Dun Cow*) and the *Yellow Book of Lecan,* says of Lady Gregory's work that she, though making "only a paraphrase," gave the "best idea of the Ulster stories." At the same time he regrets that she refined away the "coarse elements" of the stories and rationalized what was originally "monstrous and gigantesque." The bowdlerization Lady Gregory defended to a worried Yeats by insisting that it was slight. She was, I think, correct in this. Her rationalization of the monstrous is more noticeable, and here her explanation is less satisfactory:

> I have sometimes tried to give the meaning of a formula that has lost its old meaning. Thus I have exchanged for the grotesque accounts of Cuchulain's distortion—which no doubt merely meant that in time of great strain or anger he had more than human strength—the more simple formula that his appearance changed to the appearance of a god.

Right or wrong, and it reflects, I think, a mistaken view of metaphor, her decision here expresses her artistic temperament. Her own tastes are for the spare and simple. Within the bounds of her own capacity for mythmaking, she is a kind of realist. The fantastic, even in her wonder plays, is never hyperbolic, nor is her expression of its existence flamboyant. Her characters are people, not gods. She is rarely an inventor of metaphorical flights, except in the mouths of certain of her dramatic characters, and such speeches are designed to give the illusion, at least, of common speech, not authorial power or assertion of a personal imagination.

Lady Gregory did not herself employ any of the

Cuchulain stories for her plays. No doubt she considered that this was Yeats's territory. A.E., Yeats, and Synge all dramatized the legend of Deirdre. She tended, at least in the beginning of her career, to attempt plays that would fill a void.

Her *Gods and Fighting Men* followed upon *Cuchulain*. Again she consulted the available texts, the works of scholarship, and the people of the West for variants. The stories themselves combine to create a quite different impression, though her techniques remain the same. The tone is nostalgic and emphasizes decline rather than exploit. We are witness first to the descent under the earth of the Tuatha de Danaan and the subsequent wearing away of the Fianna until only aged Oisin remains. It falls on him to take the part of this ancient civilization in its dialogue with the new world, represented by St. Patrick:

> OISIN: You say that a generous man never goes to the hell of pain; there was not one among the Fianna that was not generous to all.
>
> Ask of God, Patrick, does He remember when the Fianna were alive, or has He seen east or west any man better than themselves in their fighting.
>
> The Fianna used not to be saying treachery; we never had the name of telling lies. By truth and the strength of our hands we came safe out of every battle.
>
> There never sat a priest in a church though you think it sweet to be singing psalms, was better to his word than the Fianna, or more generous than Finn himself.
>
> If my comrades were living to-night, I would take no pleasure in your crooning in the church; as they are not living now, the rough voice of the bells has deafened me.

Later Patrick breaks in:

> PATRICK: Stop your talk, you withered, witless old man;
> it is my King that made the Heavens, it is He that
> gives blossom to the trees, it is He made the moon
> and the sun, the fields and the grass.
> OISIN: It was not in shaping fields and grass that my king
> took his delight, but in overthrowing fighting men,
> and defending countries, and bringing his name into
> every part.

And:

> OISIN: I am the last of the Fianna, great Oisin, son of
> Finn, listening to the voice of bells; it is long the
> clouds are over me to-night!

Lady Gregory does not sentimentalize these tales,
though it would be easy enough to do so. Her firm
style retains an appropriate austerity. Yeats's preface
praises *Cuchulain* excessively and does not serve Lady
Gregory's effort well when it suggests that she has done
the job of translation once and for all. Nevertheless,
its conclusion reflects the spirit of cultural nationalism
in which the work was done: "If we will but tell these
stories to our children the Land will begin again to
be a Holy Land, as it was before men gave their hearts
to Greece and Rome and Judea."

Lady Gregory chose only one theme from *Gods and
Fighting Men* for a play. It was the story of Diarmuid
and Grania, attempted not very successfully by Yeats
and George Moore. There has been some speculation
about why Lady Gregory never permitted *Grania* (written 1911) to be played. Lennox Robinson reports that
she could not find satisfactory actors; others have suggested that there was something too near self-por-
traiture in it. She, herself, writes of it in a way that
invites speculation:

> I think I turned to Grania because so many have written
> about sad, lovely Deirdre, who when overtaken by sorrow

made no good battle at the last. Grania had more power
of will, and for good or evil twice took the shaping of
her life into her own hands. The riddle she asks us
through the ages is, "Why did I, having left great grey-
haired Finn for comely Diarmuid, turn back to Finn
in the end, when he had consented to Diarmuid's death?"
And a question tempts one more than the beaten path
of authorised history.

It is partly to deal with this question that Lady
Gregory has shaped her action and has deviated from
the syncretic version of the story presented in *Gods and
Fighting Men*. There the story quite naturally mean-
ders, covering numerous adventures inappropriate to
a dramatic structure. It was necessary, no matter what
her theme, to reduce the tales to an essence. In the
syncretic version Finn, now past middle age, chooses
to take a wife and is impressed by Grania's quickness
and wit. No doubt Grania is anxious to marry a man
of his eminence, but she thinks him too old and does
not care for him. Their initial conversation takes the
form of a verbal test:

they talked together for a while, and Finn was putting
questions to Grania, for she had the name of being very
quick with answers. "What is whiter than snow?" he
said. "The truth," said Grania. "What is the best colour?"
said Finn. "The colour of childhood," said she. "What
is hotter than fire?" "The face of a hospitable man when
he sees a stranger coming in, and the house empty." "What
has a taste more bitter than poison?" "The reproach of
an enemy." "What is best for a champion?" "His doings
to be high, and his pride to be low." "What is the best
of jewels?" "A knife." "What is sharper than a sword?"
"The wit of a woman between two men." "What is
quicker than the wind?" said Finn then. "A woman's
mind," said Grania. And indeed she was telling no lie
when she said that.

This is an important passage because it presents the character of Grania as quick, strong, and willful. In her play, Lady Gregory omits the episode. At its outset Grania is a more naïve and conventionally romantic heroine, even though she does take the "shaping of her life into her own hands" by her advances to Diarmuid. Of course, Lady Gregory writes with the legend in the background. We know that before Finn sought her Grania had turned down many suitors and that she has come to him by choice.

In the legend, when Diarmuid appears, the supernatural love spot on his forehead is accidentally uncovered, and Grania is immediately enchanted. She places him under Druid bonds to protect her from marriage with Finn. A most reluctant Diarmuid accepts the bonds. Eventually, after years of hiding from Finn's relentless search and of Diarmuid's refusing to sleep with her out of loyalty to Finn, a quarrel erupts between them. A visiting Fomorian "from over the western ocean in a curragh" defeats Diarmuid at chess and demands Grania as his trophy: ". . . and he put his arms about her as if to bring her away. And Grania said: 'I am this long time going with the third best man of the Fianna, and he never came as near as that to me!' " Angered and perhaps humiliated, as was Grania's intent, Diarmuid kills the Fomorian, quarrels with Grania, reconciles with her, sleeps with her that night and afterwards. Subsequently, Diarmuid is killed hunting a fabulous boar. Finn has the opportunity by a magic power accorded him to save Diarmuid's life, but jealousy intervenes each time he makes the attempt. After Diarmuid's death Grania long rejects Finn's advances, "but all the same, he went on giving her gentle talk and loving words, till in the end he brought her to his own will."

Una Ellis-Fermor, who thinks that the play loses much that is potentially dramatic in the legend, justly points out that Lady Gregory cannot include all the epic background, which establishes the recessional theme of the decline of the Fianna, partly represented by Finn's gradual aging. She feels also that without this background Finn may seem only a jealous, absurd old man. She complains that Grania and Diarmuid are conventionalized into a "bewildered girl overpowered by love" and a "chivalrous and protecting man." It is true that something of Grania's force and Finn's clever strength is lost when Lady Gregory does not exploit the possibilities of Finn's riddling questions and Grania's bright answers. At the same time something is gained by pushing Grania's first sight of Diarmuid back into her childhood, thus playing down the supernatural, and treating the occurrence as vaguely remembered. This is more dramatically credible. The emphasis on the love spot will do in the epic, but it cannot carry the full responsibility for the emotions of a character who is consistently given, in Northrop Frye's terms, a "low mimetic" credibility.

Finn's questioning of Grania reveals his fears and jealousy, for he asks her at once whether she has ever been in love. The early experience she mentions—an unknown young man (Diarmuid) separating some fighting hounds below her window and all the time full of gay laughter—seems little enough:

FINN: Did they not tell you his name?
GRANIA: I was shy to ask them, and I never saw him again. But my thoughts went with him for a good while, and sometimes he came through my dreams,—Is that now what you would call love?
FINN: Indeed I think it is little at all you know of it.

Finn cannot yet sense that she has resources of determination in her equal to his capacity for jealousy.

Lady Gregory substitutes a more chivalrous Diarmuid for a grudging, brave one. She also hints strongly that the loyal Diarmuid is immediately attracted to Grania —by his reticence in praising her beauty to Finn, despite Finn's probing, and in his suddenly expressed desire to be sent away. Lady Gregory does not press this point. It is as if she is pulling back from evoking the typical situation of romantic comedy, in which lovers—often at first sight—are blocked from marriage by an elderly fool. The Finn of the play is not the witty, stern riddler of the legend but a man beset by fears and quick to accuse—a man used to power, who feels it waning.

The first act of *Grania* ends with Grania's love for Diarmuid revealed, dire predictions made by Finn, and finally Diarmuid's foreshadowing speech: he will protect Grania, as she asks, but he will not marry her, though he admits his feelings for her, because he is bound by oaths to Finn: ". . . I tell you, Grania, but that I am bound to Finn by my word I have given him, and by kindnesses past counting and out of measure, it would be better to me than the riches of the whole world, you to have given me your love!" Their first kiss, given before Finn, Diarmuid says will be their last. Finn's swoon, a bit of melodrama, does the close of the act no good, but Diarmuid's last speech saves it: "Come out then to the hunting—for it is a long hunting it will be, and it is little comfort we will have from this out. For that is a man driven by anger, and that will not fail from our track so long as the three of us are in the living world." A world of conflict, jealousy, and divided loyalty is ordained as they are driven from Almhuin. The old, honored code of the Fianna is in decay. It is an innocent world of simple, thoughtless, heroic action that they must abandon. A peasant on Slieve Echtge told Lady Gregory once of the Fianna:

> Giants they were; Conan was twelve feet high, and he was the smallest. But ever since, people are getting smaller and smaller, and will till they come to the end; but they are wittier and more crafty than they were in the old days, for the giants were innocent though they were so strong.

Lady Gregory sacrificed some of Diarmuid's aloofness, Finn's cleverness, and Grania's quickness at the outset. But as the play proceeds, she develops Grania's character so that in the last, stunning act Grania fulfills the promise of power implicit in her early decisions to accept Finn and then to appeal to Diarmuid. At the end Finn, too, is revealed in more dimensions, his self-knowledge displayed to us in the final dialogues with Grania. The hint of Diarmuid's laughing gaiety is never developed, as it might have been to enforce his behavior; but in the last act, as he lies dying and puzzled that anything could have come between him and Finn, he expresses his true nature:

> FINN: I will turn back altogether, I will leave you Grania your wife, and all that might come between us from this time.
> DIARMUID: What could there be would come between us two? That would be a strange thing indeed.
> FINN: I will go, for the madness is as if gone from me; and you are my son and my darling, and it is beyond the power of any woman to put us asunder, or to turn you against me any more.
> DIARMUID: That would be a very foolish man would give up his dear master and his friend for any woman at all. (*He laughs*)

A greater tension might have been brought about in his character through the bulk of the play. Nevertheless, in some ways he is a more active agent than in the legend.

When the second act begins, the consummation of their marriage, after seven years, has occurred. Lady Gregory has dispensed with the visiting Fomorian of the legend. Instead, Diarmuid's jealousy is pricked by the so-called King of Foreign, who has surprised Grania alone and embraced her. As we see the lovers after this event, Diarmuid has come to accept their solitude. Grania, on the other hand, now hates it, and the willfulness that originally moved her to seek him out expresses itself vehemently. Accused of discontent and changeableness, she replies:

> It is not my mind that changes, it is life that changes about me. If I was content to be in hiding a while ago, now I am proud and have a right to be proud. And it is hard to nourish pride in a house having two in it only. . . . I will go, where it is not through the eyes of wild startled beasts you will be looking at me, but through the eyes of kings' sons that will be saying: "It is no wonder Diarmuid to have gone through his crosses for such a wife!"

Diarmuid is now hopelessly caught in the web of her discontent and Finn's jealous pursuit. The second act moves rapidly through the debate between the couple and the disguised Finn and leaves us poised on the brink of Diarmuid's fate, tormented as he is by Finn's subtle attacks on his honor: the King of Foreign still lives after embracing Grania.

At this point it is important to note that the play contains only three characters and has been criticized for all its talk. When Lady Gregory told Yeats that she was writing a three-act play with only three characters,

Yeats replied incredulously, "They must have a great deal to talk about." Indeed, they do, once the situation is satisfactorily developed. Considering the restrictions Lady Gregory placed upon herself, the last act is exceedingly well paced, and it is, except for the few important words of the dying Diarmuid, a dialogue between Finn and Grania. Here Finn captures our interest and some of our sympathy. His language grows in eloquence and metaphorical density; we recognize in him a depth of worldly experience and his own sense of his special place as leader of the Fianna. In an important part of the dialogue he reflects on how he has come to this moment:

> You came of your own free will to Almhuin to be my wife. And my heart went out to you there and then, and I thought there would be the one house between us, and that it was my child I would see reared on your knee. And that was known to every one of my people and of my armies, and you were willing it should be known. And after that was it a little thing that all Ireland could laugh at the story that I, Finn, was so spent, and withered, and loathsome in a woman's eyes, that she would not stop with me in a life that was full and easy, but ran out from me to travel the roads, the same as any beggar having seven bags. And I am not like a man of the mean people, that can hide his grief and his heartbreak, bringing it to some district where he is not known, but I must live under that wrong and that insult in full sight of all, and among mockery and malicious whisperings in the mouth of those maybe that are shouting me!

He has already been humanized for us by a simple exchange with Grania as the act begins:

GRANIA: What is it has brought you here?
FINN: Foolishness brought me here, and nature.

They have both lived much under the conditions they have created. In the dialogue of Act III Grania is a worthy opponent, and Finn's jealousy is tempered by recognition of his and her proper dignity:

> FINN: . . . it is truth you are speaking, and I will not bring you away, without you will come with me of your own will.
> GRANIA: That will be when the rivers run backward.
> FINN: No, but when the tide is at the turn.

This agon might be described as a metaphorical duel, like the riddling duel of the legend. That Finn engages her and answers her thus is, I think, his subtle tribute to her worthy opposition.

The ending of the play is, of course, terrible for Grania; she must recognize that Diarmuid's devotion to Finn is greater than his devotion to her. Diarmuid dying cannot recognize or even hear her, and he turns to Finn:

> DIARMUID (*to Finn*) : There was some word I had to say meeting you—it is gone—I had it in my mind a while ago.
> GRANIA: Do you not see me? It is I myself am here—Grania.
> DIARMUID: Some wrong I did you, some thing past forgiving.

In an ironic turnabout it is Finn who keens Diarmuid's death, while Grania is silent and angry. The play then builds swiftly to focus upon Grania's decision to go with Finn, for the tide *has* turned. She will not grieve; Finn cautions that she should wait before deciding what to do, but she does not. Partly, she wishes revenge on Diarmuid's ghost, but more deeply, she must make her life again. Because she is strong she will make it even in the face of the laughing scorn of Finn's troops. This decision is beautifully framed by Finn's speech, in which he submits to the fate he has imagined for their lives and also indicates why the play has only three characters:

> we three have been these seven years as if alone in the world. . . . And now there are but the two of us left, and whether we love or hate one another, it is certain I can never feel love or hatred for any other woman from this out, or you yourself for any other man. And so as to yourself and myself, Grania, we must battle it out to the end.

Unlike Finn and Diarmuid, who both submitted in some way to the conditions of their lives, Grania does not submit. She passes through derisive laughter to a new life:

> (*She opens the door herself. Finn puts his arm about her. There is another great peal of laughter, but it stops suddenly as she goes out.*)

When all is said, this play is a study of a woman. It is tempting to speculate on Lady Gregory's own interest in her play. She was certainly fascinated by Grania's capacity to act. With this came the problem of remorse. Grania's remorselessness is perhaps a reflection of that opposite Yeats delighted to imagine Lady Gregory's seeking in her art. One senses in Lady Gregory a highly ethical code, a considerable capacity for remorse coupled with power of invention and will to action. She was well aware that in the working out of the implications of Grania's personal power there is a price. If Grania is truly alive at the end, there is also something austere and a little terrible about the qualities in her that protect her from despair. Yeats's poem to Lady Gregory on the occasion of her failure to obtain an art gallery for Dublin concerns itself with this theme, which, one suspects, he considers central to her character: "Bred to a harder thing / Than Triumph," she is advised to "Be secret and exult."

Lady Gregory wrote that her first tragedy, *Kincora* (1905, revised 1909), was on the subject of Brian Boru, the High King who defeated the Danes at Clontarf in 1014. But the play is also, if not principally, the study of a woman. Queen Gormleith moves the action. It is a more sprawling play than *Grania,* and Lady Gregory rewrote it at least once with the help of both Yeats and Synge. Fundamentally, the play expresses the clash of Queen Gormleith's will to action with the elderly Brian's desire to forsake arms and impose unification and peace upon Ireland. Through her restless pride Gormleith is a stirrer-up of strife:

> MAELMORA: Brian is surely getting a great name of piety to put along with his name of riches and of power; having, as he has, his head in the skies, and his hand in every good work.
>
> GORMLEITH: Where is the use of gaining power if you go turn from it after to shadows?

In the end she takes credit, through her treachery, for bringing about the impending battle of Clontarf, which will give Brian his place in history but which he will not survive. There is some momentary remorse on her part, but it is slight by comparison to her feeling that she has created a hero. She is a sort of mythmaker. Brian is dismayed that his hopes for peace have been thwarted:

MALACHI: Look at the work you have done. (*He points to Brian*) Go out and hang your head for shame. The man that was steady and strong is broken. It is hardly he will reach to the battle.

GORMLEITH: No fear, no fear, Brian will reach to the battle. There is no fear at all of him not doing that. It is not Brian would wish to die the death of a man that is lessening and stiffening, the time he grows attentive to his bed, but of a winner that is merry and shouting, the time his enemies are put down. I was maybe a right wife for him. A right wife, a lucky wife, in spite of all!

There is a hint of Gormleith's satisfaction after the fact here, and it makes her far less attractive than Grania. In the first version of the play the ending is hers as she exults in having made Brian a hero. In the final version the ending is Brian's as he realizes he will make history at Clontarf. The emphasis on Gormleith's act is lessened, and there is a curious falling off, for Gormleith is not present as the play ends, and she has dominated the play to that point. The first version was slow in its early stages, the second blurs its focus at the end.

Lady Gregory's third tragedy of mythological history is the one-act *Dervorgilla* (1907), where remorse is all. In a note she describes the historical circumstance:

Dervorgilla, daughter of the King of Meath, wife of O'Rourke, King of Breffny, was taken away, willingly or unwillingly by Diarmuid MacMurrough, King of Leinster, in the year 1152. O'Rourke and his friends invaded Leinster in revenge, and in the wars which followed, Diarmuid, driven from Ireland, appealed for help to Henry II of England, and was given an army under Strongbow, to whom Diarmuid promised Leinster as reward. It is so the English were first brought into Ireland.

Dervorgilla is, then, responsible for this event. The play is a simple one in which the old woman, living incognito in Mellifont Abbey, must face still another tragedy wrought by the English presence, during which her identity is revealed to those to whom she has made gifts. The play was one of Lennox Robinson's favorites, "a small masterpiece." Thematically, it differs from the treatment of Grania and Gormleith, in that Dervorgilla, no matter what her original motives and control over events, suffers deep remorse.

Lady Gregory's mythological history, stretching in these three plays from the time of Finn to the coming of the English, casts women in the pivotal roles. But more important, we learn that history is made out of fundamental human relationships, of the clash of wills, of the passions of domestic life. Her mythological history rips the veil of the high romantic and reveals a dialogue between husband and wife, a hearth and those who keep it or defile it. Her kings and warriors walk our earth, live in houses or are banished from them, and argue with their wives. Her heroines are those who "meddle," who would drive their men or assert their own wills, challenge destiny for better or worse, and live with the results. An old ironic saying tells us that the Irish were all kings once. Lady Gregory's myth tells us the kings were people, and that they had wives. Her plays are expressions of a humanized mythology that grew from the life around her, but that gave back something too—the vision of great things happening among a simple and long-oppressed people.

In *Our Irish Theatre,* Lady Gregory revealed her vision "of historical plays being sent by us through all the counties of Ireland. For to have a real success and to come into the life of the country, one must touch a real and eternal emotion, and history comes only next to religion in our country." Irish history was for long forbidden in the schools and was therefore learned mostly from the works of poets like Raftery. She says in *Poets and Dreamers* of his poems: "It is hard to say where history ends in them and religion and politics begin."

Lady Gregory's tragedies, as we have observed, are not what might be called "high tragedies." Even the basic situation at the outset of *Grania* might have been one of comedy. Her mythological history plays, whether inhabited by kings or peasants, set themselves in a world familiar to or readily imaginable to the inhabitants of, say, County Galway. Even kings and heroes seem conceived as not higher than we, but about the same. Indeed, the tragedies of Grania, Gormleith, and Dervorgilla do not end in death for these women, but for the men involved with them. The women must make new lives out of their own capacities to exert will. In at least one of these plays there is a sort of upturning, not of fortune but of renewed self-mastery. The plays all stress the quality of endurance, which is not surprising, considering Lady Gregory's own life and character and her sense of Ireland's past and present, which seemed to require that she make a myth of endurance.

The two plays, *The Canavans* (1906) and *The White Cockade* (1905), which she called both folk-history plays and tragic comedies, are in the tradition of Raftery's poetic history. They are the sort of comedy that rises from oppression. The foolishness, with its pathetic undertones, is spread equally among tyrants and oppressed, and scorn falls most heavily upon puffery and cowardice. The plays are in a limited sense "didactic."

Grania and *Kincora* reach into a mythological past and offer models of heroic behavior and an analysis of the wages of strength. The tragic comedies would seem to take a historically verifiable condition—oppression—and examine the follies of a people too long under it. Split loyalty and the clash between loyalty and expedience are central issues.

In *The Canavans* the tragedy is very much an undertone that exists merely in the state of affairs that makes a Peter Canavan possible. Lady Gregory wrote about it, "The desire possessing Peter Canavan to be on the safe side, on the side of the strongest, is not bounded by any century or kept within the borders of any country, though it jumps to light more aggressively in one which, like Ireland, has been tilted between two loyalties through so many generations." The play is based more on folklore than any written record and has the playfulness of a story elaborated as it goes along. This is particularly so in the farcical business of Antony Canavan's effecting his escape from jail by impersonating Queen Elizabeth and fooling not only his captors but his ridiculous brother. The turnabout at the end of the play, when the cowardly, self-serving Peter prates of his newly found strength and courage, is ironic, since his cowardice is merely exchanged for braggadocio based on illusion and has no more substance than his loyalty.

In *The White Cockade,* which brings Lady Gregory's mythological history up to the time of James II and the Battle of the Boyne, Patrick Sarsfield is the hero deeply loyal to an Ireland powerless to help itself. He cannot find a human object upon which to fix that loyalty. James is Catholic, but he is not Irish and is a coward. There is nowhere else to turn, so Sarsfield

attempts to move James to actions of which he is in-
capable. Sarsfield is an idealist, but in the end his
idealism, wounded by James's defection, appears madness to those around him, including a dotty old lady
who has had great hopes for James. Lady Gregory's
note on the play says:

> In these days, when so much of the printed history we
> were taught as children is being cast out by scholars, we
> must refill the vessel by calling in tradition, or if need
> be our own imaginings. When my *White Cockade* was
> first produced I was pleased to hear that J. M. Synge had
> said my method had made the writing of historical drama
> again possible.

Split loyalty, betrayal by the crown, internal wrangling when the moment for action arises, incredible
bad luck or bad planning—these have all been historical
facts of Irish politics and nationalist movements. An
aura of what-might-have-been hangs over such reminiscences. Yeats remarked that someone once said to him
that Ireland would never have a future because it had
a present; and Wilde remarked that the Irish were the
greatest talkers since the Greeks, a nation of brilliant
failures. In *The Canavans* the talk turns into silly
posturing. In *The Wrens* (1914) the verbalizing of
the characters outside the Irish parliament in 1799
becomes a mad parody of the debate over dissolution
inside. Strangely and ironically, the parody—the external wrangling—so catches up the attention of the
servant of a leading nationalist that he fails to notify
him that the final vote is about to be taken. The
result is a vote lost by one ballot, the dissolution of
the Irish parliament, union with England, and the end
of any semblance of home rule. At the play's outset the

servant and the porter have the following exchange, which reflects what will go on in the street and is an image of the country and its wrangling political unrest:

SERVANT: Are they making speeches yet?
PORTER: They are: Arguing and debating, Lords and Commons, through night and through dawn, till they have the world talked upside down.

The porter, a skeptic, is uncertain of the outcome of the vote; too many things of this sort have been settled by chance:

SERVANT: . . . noble and high-blooded people are against it! Languaged people that can turn history to their own hand!
PORTER: They might not. To be supple with the tongue is not all.
SERVANT: I tell you the most thing in the mighty world could not save that bill from being thrown out and refused!
PORTER: It's hard to say. There was no great strength in the wrens that destroyed Ireland the time they went picking crumbs on a drum, and wakened up the army of the Danes.

Pathetically, words are the Irish weapon. The servant's faith in them is excessive. But ironically, it is words that will bring down the parliament—words and the chance appearance of two strolling singers. The servant does not know he is prophetic when he points to them and says, "And what sort is it you are thinking will destroy the liberties of Ireland this day? Is it that couple of raggedy strollers are disputing along the side path of the Green?" Of course, it is. The two wordmongers argue between themselves over the union—the wife a Protestant nationalist, the husband a Catholic who holds that the priests support the union. The spat involves the onlookers, then turns into a wrangle about the husband's drinking. The husband agrees to take the pledge until the union bill is thrown out, thinking this is imminent. The wife then shifts her politics completely. When the vote is lost because of the servant's distraction over the quarrel, the husband is held to his pledge, the wife content, but behind it all, and nearly forgotten, the union is established.

To the student of the Easter Rising or the career of Wolfe Tone or Robert Emmet, this play carries into art the pathos of the incredible misfortunes that have plagued Irish nationalism—plans gone awry, mistaken messages, wrong turns taken in the road, intraparty squabbles, the added complexity of religious strife (which plays an ironic part here where the Catholic husband defends his unionism, citing ecclesiastical support). It is comic and it is tragic. Northrop Frye has remarked that if in Synge's *Riders to the Sea* each death actually occurred during the play—all being virtually the same—the audience would be helpless with laughter by the end. Something of that sort of absurdity Lady Gregory capitalizes on here. It is another tragic turn of Irish fortunes.

The theme of words is important. All the complexity of the cultural and political life of Ireland required mythmakers to bring it to shape in the imagination, for the words of political rhetoric had hopelessly clouded every issue. Yeats knew this, and wrote of it in his *Autobiography*. The *Aeolus* episode of *Ulysses* is record of Joyce's sensitivity to the matter. Lady Gregory's mythological history looks into the plight of a people, turns the coin over so that the tragedy and comedy, the image and the reality, the loyalty and the self-serving may be confronted under the pressure of history.

For her own generation, Ireland's mythological history could not be written without attention to Parnell. It is not surprising that Parnell should figure in one of Lady Gregory's plays, just as he appears in Yeats, Joyce, and other major Irish writers. It is not surprising that Lady Gregory should examine the turning against Parnell in an allegory. It was perhaps too close to her, too much a historical reality to be faced head on. In any case her play *The Deliverer* (1911), though written in the Kiltartan dialect, is set in Egypt in the time of the Pharaohs. The allegory is a very thin veil, the story hardly more than invective. The betrayal of Parnell, like the murder of Kennedy or King for Americans, is more than Lady Gregory was able to handle in her usually straightforward, low mimetic style.

Her mythological history comes more successfully into times recent to her writing in *The Gaol Gate* (1906) and *The Rising of the Moon* (published 1904). These plays are concerned with loyalty, divided or pure. *The Gaol Gate,* her favorite among her tragedies, is a four-page, one-act play that tells a story suitable to a poetic ballad. A mother and her daughter-in-law are outside the jail where her son is incarcerated under accusation of murder done by others. They are wracked by fear that he will die for it but also that he will inform. When they learn of his death, for they are too late to see him, they grieve, but the wife speaks with pride, reasserting the code of a people under a foreign law. He has not informed.

The Rising of the Moon is a well-made one-act play in which the issue is a policeman's loyalty to his duty conflicting with his nationalistic spirit, brought to fervor by the singing of an old ballad by a fugitive he is supposed to capture. Lady Gregory's own note best describes its effect:

> The play was considered offensive to some extreme Nationalists before it was acted, because it showed the police in too favourable a light, and a Unionist paper attacked it after it was acted because the policeman was represented "as a coward and a traitor"; but after the Belfast police strike that same paper praised its "insight into Irish character."

Irish dramatists who wished finally to explore an issue rather than paint it black or white frequently faced attack. Yeats's *Countess Cathleen* upset some amateur theologians and some bishops. Synge's *Playboy* offended a variety of people. Lady Gregory's plays had few obviously controversial aspects, but under the surface farce of many of her plays she eyes the Irish predicament, writes the history of the Irish soul, which is a mythological history—the soul not being, any more than the fabulous Sidhe, content to wait upon fact.

The tendency of those who would make or restore a mythology to a people, as Lady Gregory sought to do with her *Cuchulain, Gods and Fighting Men*, and many plays, is likely to be conservative—to look back upon past heroism and to honor received tradition. But in her time and place, though conservative in this sense, her work was revolutionary, for it was an attempt to establish the grounds for political and religious freedom—a freedom that cannot even be imagined without the establishment of some constantly sought ideal image and the perpetuation of self-criticism. Her telling of the ancient stories and her tragedies seek to imply the image; the comedies to which we now turn puncture false images, tell all.

3
Cloon

What now remains of Coole Park is two miles north of the small market-town of Gort, which lies on the border between Counties Clare and Galway about half-way between Ennis and Galway city. Muirhead's *Guide* describes Gort as a "clean but dull little town, with a large triangular market-place." The Irish Tourist Board is more charitable, calling it "pleasant," but adding nothing more. In truth it is a gray western village with an ugly Catholic church, an empty Protestant one, two small hotels of no distinction, and typical storefronts facing on a marketplace. The Gort workhouse, which probably inspired *The Workhouse Ward,* disappeared before Lady Gregory's death. In the forty-odd years she has been gone, the town has not changed very much in outward appearance or, one suspects, inwardly. A road leads northwest to Galway, passing the turn-off for Coole. Yeats's Thoor Ballylee, now restored as a memorial, is northeast, off a less-traveled country road.

If Gort is of any special interest, that is because it resembles Lady Gregory's mythical village of Cloon. Otherwise it is totally unexceptional, but that is what

Cloon is, too—a western town where nothing in particular is likely to happen. Nor is Cloon special because
special characters have been invented to live there. Some
of Lady Gregory's characters inhabit more than one
of her plays, but except for Hyacinth Halvey, who appears in both the play named for him and *The Full
Moon,* these characters do not dominate the plays. They
are present not in order to emphasize their own odysseys
but to fill out a world possessing a degree of universality.
Lady Gregory also tended to see her plays first as pictures. The stage setting for *Hyacinth Halvey* would
seem to contain a seed of the subsequent action, as if
the action were saying to us that *this* is, in movement,
what the picture had meant.

Lady Gregory's use of character in her comedies is
far from romantic; it is classical. She would subscribe
to the Aristotelian view that character is present for
the purpose of the action. In some ultimate sense, however, for her the action is there to present the static
image of a world. One imagines that with the conclusion of one of her actions and with, say, the next
morning's opening of the shops in Cloon square, all
things and all people will be at the places appointed
them in the original stage directions. This is obvious
in such shorter plays as *The Workhouse Ward* and
Coats, least obvious but equally true in *Spreading the
News,* where at the play's end certain things remain
to be cleared up among the characters before the original situation is restored. *The Workhouse Ward* (1908)
has the quality of a tableau that is for a little while
interrupted by a minor crisis resolved ironically. It
invites a brief meditation on its scene—two old paupers
endlessly wrangling in their separate beds. It is not
surprising that Lady Gregory herself meditated upon

the scene and observed, "I sometimes think the two scolding paupers are a symbol of ourselves in Ireland— 'It is better to be quarrelling than to be lonesome.' " *Coats* (1910) offers the picture of two rival newspaper editors lunching at the Royal Hotel, Cloonmore. The action of the play is a confused argument between them over their respective obituary notices. It breaks the quiet of their lives, but is resolved. One imagines them sitting there again at the next noon, the next argument on another subject, but again resolved. Lady Gregory's plays are very Irish, but they arise out of a conception that life is everywhere fundamentally the same and that the fundamentals do not change from age to age. This is the attitude of the folklorist and of one who is conscious of a tradition and seeking to preserve or restore it. Finally, it is one of an artist observing a society that has been conservative, isolated, and jealous of its privacy, suspicious of the invader.

The restoration of order is, of course, conventional to comedy. The society of comedy protects its norms, purging outrageous behavior, often embodied by a ridiculous figure like Molière's miser or his hypochondriac. Social forms and sensible behavior, including romantic love, will be endorsed, dangerous foolishness abolished, and trivial foolishness tolerated within bounds. Lady Gregory was a great admirer of Molière and translated four of his plays for Abbey performance, but though she certainly must have learned a great deal from a study of his plots, it is not plot that she mentions in a note on *The Doctor in Spite of Himself*. What struck her was its similarity to a folk tale:

One of the Dublin papers was shocked at the roughness and simplicity of the Play, and the writer of the article, although he admitted he had never read Molière's text, accused us of putting these things into it. Now it is precisely this roughness and simplicity, as of some old humorous folk-tale, that has made it a world-famous masterpiece, for it can be translated into almost any language, or adapted into any social order that is not too complex.

Her own plots differ from Molière's. One is never certain that the order she has restored ought to be greeted with much approbation. One is not certain that there has been any decisive victory over the forces of ridiculousness. In *Spreading the News* (1904) the source of disturbance lies not in one person's aberration. Rather, the play describes an apparently unaccountable upheaval that we suspect will die down only to arise again like a cyclic natural occurrence. Neither is the order observed with bitter irony as an evil indestructible oppression bound to triumph. Instead, the perspective of the creator of this world is ironically loving; things simply are as they are, people are as they are. All will remain much as it is. The difference from Molière's plots is that the "humour" restricted in Molière to one character, by and large, spreads rapidly or is always latent in the whole of Lady Gregory's society. At the same time her world, no matter what its universality, springs from a specific place, which has its own mythological history.

The characters of Cloon first appear in Lady Gregory's early comedy *Spreading the News*. The opening scene presents us with the "outskirts of a Fair. An Apple Stall." The only reference to Cloon is a casual remark about the graveyard at Cloonmara, but two of the people, Bartley Fallon and Shawn Early, are Cloon residents in the later *Full Moon* (1910) and the situation is one perfectly in keeping with that of *The Jackdaw* (written 1902, revised 1907) and *Hyacinth Halvey* (1906), which are set in the town itself. The plot is a typically complicated one of mistaken understanding and exuberant fancy, moved along by the constant misinterpretations of what others have said by the deaf proprietress of the apple stall, Mrs. Tarpey. Citizens, policeman, and magistrate all fail to escape the flow of erroneous news. Indeed, they create from the misinterpretations an outlandish tale of infidelity, jealous anger, and murder that places poor Bartley Fallon in handcuffs. Each person makes his misinterpretations in different ways: Mrs. Tarpey is merely deaf; the magistrate is insensitive, endlessly referring his present experience to what happened to him in his previous duty "in the Andaman Islands" and never really seeing the reality around him; the policeman is a mindless flunky who can only mechanically endorse with repetition the magistrate's remarks; Tim Casey leaps exuberantly to conclusions; Shawn Early is gullible. Each in his own way is as deaf as Mrs. Tarpey, who is always present to add confusion to fiction. In the midst of this is poor, sad Fallon, who would go to America but fears he would die there without the money for a decent burial, and lives constantly bemoaning his ill fortune. Of course, there has been no infidelity, no murder—only talk; but as the play ends, Fallon and his supposed victim, Jack Smith, are led away to jail, the magistrate convinced that they have concealed a body and that everybody is lying. One knows that there will be an unravelment, though not without further confusions. Events will play themselves out, leaving things pretty much as they were. The virus will die down, but Mrs. Tarpey is clearly a "carrier" and there is no permanent immunity. Also, one comes to think that the people have actually found exhilaration in their confusion.

Lady Gregory must have had considerable pleasure writing a note about this play in the Abbey Theatre magazine, *The Arrow,* finding again in one of her works a symbolism after the fact:

> Some time ago at a debate in Dublin a speaker complained that the Irish peasantry were slandered in *Spreading the News,* because nowhere in Ireland would so improbable a story grow out of so little; and in the same speech he said our Theatre was not worthy of support, because we "had given our first performance at the Castle." Another speaker pointed to this fiction as a very Spreading of the News. Since that day it has been said of us that we never play but in Irish, that our Theatre is "something done for the Roman Catholics," that it has been "got up by the Irish Parliamentary Party with Mr. Healy at the head of them," that we have a special fee of fifty pounds a performance for anybody from Trinity College who wishes to hire the Theatre, that our "attitude toward the Irish peasant arises out of class prejudice which keeps us from seeing anything that is good in him." . . . Some at least of these accusations must be founded on evidence as airy as that given in the case of the murder of Jack Smith.

In *Spreading the News* no scapegoat is driven out; there are no characters who obtain our sympathy as frustrated, then reconciled lovers. Fallon, who finds gloom equally in the prospects of early death or long life, is a random victim for a while, and the whole of the society shares in the responsibility for events. The range of that society, as we see it developed through *Hyacinth Halvey* and *The Jackdaw* to *The Full Moon,* is enclosed by extremes. At one end of the scale are the fools of *The Full Moon,* Cracked Mary and her innocent brother, Davideen. At the other is Halvey, the naïve young man over from Carrow who, in obtaining character references for himself, is forced by the townfolk to be the exemplary person the letters say he is. The people between are the sane fools or foolish sane—the paupers, shopkeepers, and professional people who spread the news. Their characteristics are commonly the following:

1. A stubborn, virtually conspiratorial resistance to governmental authority, which is always considered alien. In *Hyacinth Halvey* Mrs. Delane, the postmistress, delays a telegram to Sergeant Carden to frustrate his search for tainted meat in Mr. Quirke's shop. Magistrate and policeman in *Spreading the News* live in their own worlds, partly as a result of their own doggedly narrow imaginations, also because the townsfolk are never prepared to speak directly to their questions or to assist them in any way. Mrs. Tarpey answers the magistrate's question about what the town's chief business is by saying, "minding one another's business." This, as it turns out, is Mrs. Tarpey's one accurate piece of news, but it is lost to the magistrate's one-track mind and is really an evasion on her part. In best sleuthing parlance he says, "I shall learn nothing here," thus missing the clue.

2. A certain isolation in the self. This quality has been noticed by Ann Saddlemyer. There is a curious lack of contact among the citizens at the level of what we may call rationally perceived reality. Where there is a common reality it is *built up,* not of fact but disregard for fact, and is therefore transitory and fragile and ever-changing while it stands, though, as I have suggested, much enjoyed.

3. Exuberance in disregard for fact. The world of Cloon has for us two existences, the people whom we observe from our citadel of reason, the armchair or theater seat, and the world of rumor and "improvement" on their lives that the people create about themselves often to

the point that it has a life of its own and begins to control theirs, as a myth will do. Lady Gregory mentioned in connection with *The Bogie Men* "our incorrigible genius for myth-making, the faculty that makes our traditional history a perpetual joy, because it is, like the Sidhe, an eternal Shape-changer." Each of her comedies might be thought of as a seed or an image or a chance phrase that in the minds of those who pass it among themselves grows, like Cuchulain in battle, into a wonder or a monster. It is strange, considering Lady Gregory's interest in the exuberance of her characters' imaginations in Cloon, that she should have rationalized the descriptions of Cuchulain that she translated. (For an example of exuberance there one must go to another translation, that of Thomas Kinsella.) But Lady Gregory does find in her townspeople the same exuberance the authors of the *Tain* had. One of these, Bartley Fallon, begins *The Full Moon* his sane sad self, grows with the myth of the mad dog into a sad rabid man, appears finally with a chicken crate over his head to protect those he thinks he may attack when the madness comes upon him, as he is now certain it will. Yet in the end the supposedly mad dog, who has not bitten Fallon, metamorphoses back into Peter Tannion's pet, who has merely stolen a piece of meat from Mr. Quirke's cart and is chased by boys. In *The Jackdaw* Mr. Nestor, who likes to read the gossip news, invents an outlandish story on the moment to get out of a tight spot, and it is believed and then embellished by the townspeople. The question one might ask is: What is Cloon without these disrupting improvisations on the thin surface of reality? A dull place, surely. A place would be bringing on the madness!

4. The tendency to build images, ideals, or romantic visions. Lady Gregory's favorite among her plays was apparently her tragic comedy *The Image* (1909), a rather slow play in places, I fear, but clearly involving an idea central to her work. As she herself points out, each character has an image in his mind, a "heart-secret" that is in some sense an illusion. Each of these secrets is exploded as the play proceeds, for each is fragile, and "the more ecstatic the vision the more impossible its

realisation." Lady Gregory's own note to the play is
self-ironic, reflecting upon what she implies is one of
her own "heart-secrets." She remarks that it has been
said of the play: ". . . this is what Lady Gregory calls a
comedy, but everybody else calls a farce." Thus she
ironically appears to reveal and destroy her own secret,
except that if Lady Gregory's plays are farces, then we
must agree to new distinctions, for she imbeds in the
conventions of farce a constant *attitude,* a pathos, and a
love.

The plot of *The Image* is typically full of misunder-
standings and conclusions exuberantly built upon them.
The citizens of a western seacoast village learn that
two whales have been washed up on the beach and
begin to discuss how to spend the money that the oil
from these beasts will bring them. It is decided that
it will be spent in the erection of a statue to some
substantial person. After much argument and consid-
eration of such names as O'Connell and Parnell, the
people choose to commemorate a man named Hugh
O'Lorrha. This name has been proposed by Malachi
Naughton, who on the night before had experienced
numerous wonderful things: strange noises, the pre-
mature crowing of a cock, the birth of two kids from
his goat, and the three goats subsequently discovered
on the beach munching at a board on which the name
Hugh O'Lorrha is painted. At once O'Lorrha becomes
Malachi's heart-secret:

> There should be some meaning in it and some message.
> No doubt about it at all, it was a night full of wonders—
> Down in the tide there to be the noise as of hundreds,
> the bird in the rafters making its own outcry, and its
> call—the goat to be bringing me to that bit of a board
> —Hugh O'Lorrha, that should be a very high sounding

name. What it is at all he is calling to me, and bidding me for to do?

The name actually belongs to a Kerry man whose boat has been lost in the same storm that beached the whales. Malachi Naughton's vision of his heroic mythical man is eventually challenged, and he answers: "Take care but it was no dream! Let you go out looking yourself so in the night time. And if you do go, it is likely you will see nothing but the flaggy rocks and the clefts, for it's not all are born to see things of the kind. I'll tell you no more, I wish I had told you nothing. . . ." As the pressure upon his vision becomes greater he chooses the vision rather than the society:

> Oh, my heart-secret, wait till I'll hide you from them all, and they not able to understand a thing they are not fit to understand! There's a bad class of people in this place, are not worthy to see so much as your name! I don't want to be annoyed with them any more than I am. I'll keep my knowledge to myself, between myself and the bare stones. I'll go back to the beasts and the birds that pay respect to him!

This is not the speech of pure comedy or of farce. It is too desperate and too personal. Malachi may be a fool, but there is pathos in his foolishness.

There is nothing communal about the secrets of the characters in *The Image* except that separate secrets are brought together by events and interwoven each with the other. When Lady Gregory focuses upon the separateness she produces her tragic comedies; when the communal world is built from the images, and that world submerges the characters and gains a life of its own, there is comedy.

The Image contains a range of heart-secrets from the heroic to the more personal and simple. In every case, however, the image is badly battered when it is made available to the skepticism and scoffing of others. Malachi Naughton and Peggy Mahon are outraged at the fate of their heart-secrets at the hands of their neighbors. Yet others are oddly relieved. The stonemason Coppinger, who was to have the great opportunity to make the statue of Malachi's hero, is not finally forced to bring the image to the light of day, thus either destroying it by making it public, or failing to do its ideality justice.

> COSTELLO: Let you not fret, Thomas. There did no badness of misfortune ever come upon Ireland but someone was the better of it. You not to go shape the image, there is no person can say, it is to mis-shape it you did. Let you comfort yourself this time, for it is likely you would have failed doing the job.
> COPPINGER: I was thinking that myself, Darby. I to begin I'd have to follow it up, and the deer knows where might it leave me.

Something of the primitive sense of the independent power of the word is the subject of Lady Gregory's play and is emphasized at the end when Peggy Mahon rejects Coppinger's offer to put a stone with her husband's name over his grave: "I'll ask no headstone and his name upon it, and strangers maybe to be sounding it out with the queer crabbed talk they have, and the gibberish, and ridiculing it, and maybe making out my clean comrade, my comely Patrick, to be but a blemished little maneen, having a stuttering tongue." The ancient Irish fear of the power of the poet's satire as spell lives on here. But there is another side to the power of words, enunciated by the play's last speaker:

"We'll not be scarce of talk for the rest of our years anyway. For some do be telling the story was always in it, but we will be telling the story never was in it before and never will be in it at all!" Myth triumphs over reality; it must do so, for without the myth created and sustained even for a short time, people have nothing at all. Reason and reality can press upon it, and even cause a change in the myth, but do not succeed in substituting an imaginative void.

Yet one can be trapped by a myth that conflicts with one's own heart-secret. Into the town of Cloon comes young Hyacinth Halvey, the new Sub-Sanitary Inspector, armed with countless character references, all written in extravagant praise by people he barely knows. The citizens wish him to be what the written word says. They engage a room for him convenient to the police barracks and into which the curate can see from his window:

HYACINTH: I think maybe I'd best look around a bit before I'll settle in a lodging—
MISS JOYCE: Not at all. *You* won't be wanting to pull down the blind.
MRS. DELANE: It is not likely *you* will be snaring rabbits.
MISS JOYCE: Or bringing in a bottle and taking an odd glass the way James Kelly did.

And on they go, imagining him spending his evenings learning O'Growney's exercises, sticking postcards in an album for the convent bazaar, reading *The Catholic Young Man* and *The Lives of the Saints,* playing the melodeon, until finally he cries out in anguish, "I wish I had never seen Cloon." After this his desperate efforts to do something to tarnish his "character" turn farcically into good works, and the play ends with a protesting Halvey being chaired through the town to deliver a lecture on "The Building of Character," the scheduled speaker having missed the train.

The fate of poor Halvey differs from the fate of others in Lady Gregory's comedies in that the news spread about him dogs him relentlessly right to the end of the action. He is not a Molièrean "humour" who deserves, we decide, our raillery, and there is thus something uneasy about the situation in which the man is left. Poor Halvey cannot glory in the role given him, as does Christy Mahon in Synge's *Playboy*. He is not an outcast or rebel by nature. We see him last caught up and carried like a hero into a myth that seems almost now his destiny, such is the power of the society about him and of luck to press him onward. Like Malachi Naughton and Peggy Mahon, these people need heart-secrets, and he is the material to hand. As Lady Gregory remarked, in the world she writes of, " 'character' is built up or destroyed by a password or an emotion rather than by experience or deliberation." This is Lady Gregory in a critical mood—critical of the conspiratorial air that the oppressor has forced upon Irish life, critical of the excess of emotion in such judgments as are made. The play is also, however, by the Lady Gregory who understands the need for myth-making as well as the incorrigibility of this tendency in Ireland.

As are we, Lady Gregory was uneasy about Hyacinth Halvey's fate. In a note to *The Full Moon*, she wrote: "It has sometimes preyed on my mind that Hyacinth Halvey had been left by me in Cloon for his lifetime, bearing the weight of a character that had been put on him by force." In *The Full Moon*, she contrives his escape. Ernest Boyd, whose opinion of Lady Gregory's plays was not high, disliked the resuscitation of Halvey and the Cloon characters, thinking it an example of poverty of invention. *The Full Moon* he called a play "utterly devoid of good humor." My own opinion is the opposite of Boyd's. He mistook serious comic purpose for sourness and did not see that Lady Gregory was filling out a world rather than repeating herself from a grab-bag of tricks.

We already know that Hyacinth Halvey is different from the other residents of Cloon. When Bartley Fallon is taken off to jail at the end of *Spreading the News,* we are not deeply concerned, even though he may anticipate a beating from the outraged Jack Smith. When Hyacinth Halvey is chaired through the marketplace in apparent triumph, we are woefully anxious for him. Fallon accepts the myth of the mad dog in *The Full Moon* and accepts equally its demise. Halvey does not accept it but ends the play barking. Fallon is of Cloon; Halvey belongs to us.

In the play a group of people, including Halvey and Fallon, are waiting in a shed at Cloon Station to greet the returning Father Grogan. Cracked Mary, recently back from the asylum, appears with her brother, Davideen. The evening will produce a full moon, and there is talk of madness and its causes. Cracked Mary taunts Halvey, who would like to be going to the Carrow fair. The dog runs by, chased by boys, and Cracked Mary spins a tale out of the event that leads Fallon to think himself infected, while Halvey tries to find some excuse to leave but fails. As the play proceeds, Cracked Mary's wild talk infects Halvey, and finally it is he who feigns madness to escape the shed and board the train.

Cracked Mary is perhaps a rather sad symbol of

Lady Gregory

freedom, but she serves a certain irony in the play. Lady Gregory wrote of this:

> it failed me to release him by reason, that "binds men to the wheel"; it took the call of some of those unruly ones who give in to no limitations, and dance to the sound of music that is outside this world, to bring him out from "roast and boiled and the comforts of the day." Where he is now I do not know, but anyway he is free.

The world of Cloon, as we well know, is hardly a world where reason reigns supreme, so one might possibly imagine the imposition of rationality as saving Halvey, but Lady Gregory, as calm and detached in her observations as she is, chooses otherwise. After all, one can hardly imagine a rational ordering of the society she presents. Relief from the myth comes only with adoption of a new myth, and this Cracked Mary provides in her crazed talk of the moon—the traditional "wisdom" of the mad:

> CRACKED MARY: There was a great shouting in the big round house, and you coming into it last night.
> HYACINTH HALVEY: What are you saying? I never went frolicking in the night time since the day I came into Cloon.
> CRACKED MARY: We were talking of it a while ago. I knew you by the smile and by the laugh of you. A queen having a yellow dress, and the hair on her smooth like marble. All the dead of the village were in it, and of the living myself and yourself.
> HYACINTH HALVEY: I thought it was of Carrow she was talking: it is of the other world she is raving, and of the shadows-shapes of the forth. . . .
> CRACKED MARY: Make a snap at the bridle as it passes by the bush in the western gap. Run out now, run, where you have the bare ridge of the world before

you, and no one to take orders from but yourself,
maybe, and God.

In another play, *The Bogie Men* (1912), two chimney
sweeps escape an oppressive myth that has been a
torment to each of them, but in that play, though they
achieve a sort of mental release, their outward lives are
not much changed, and one of them is skeptical of their
luck. But in *The Full Moon,* in giving Halvey his freedom, Lady Gregory takes us right to the edge of wonder.

4
Wonder

To refer to the Irishman's so-called disregard for fact and his propensity for the construction of tales of wonder is to perpetuate a cliché. Still, a folk tradition, replete with mythological creatures and wondrous events, existed and was the basis of Lady Gregory's most substantial book of folklore, *Visions and Beliefs in the West of Ireland* (1920). The Irish world of wonder is adequately represented in it. She transcribed tales of seers, healers, herbs, charms, banshees, ghosts, apparitions, monsters, sheoguey beasts, and miraculous cures. Accounts of these she renders in the Kiltartan dialect in which she was told of them.

It is interesting to observe what she reveals of her own attitudes toward these beliefs. Unlike Yeats, who sought proof in folklore for a faith in the supernatural, Lady Gregory was very careful to remain noncommittal without exhibiting skepticism. She does not try to force the tales she has heard into the context of, or a rationale for, her beliefs. She does not intrude upon the stories she reports, in contrast to Yeats, who tends to press a belief upon his reader, as if he were trying

to overcome his own skepticism. Lady Gregory seems
capable of accepting the possibility that different worlds
exist for different consciousnesses. She respects the
stories she hears and the people who tell them. Apparently with one exception, she had not experienced
events of the order that she records:

> though I had heard all my life some talk of the faeries
> and the banshee (have indeed reason to believe in this
> last), I had never thought of giving heed to what I, in
> common with my class, looked on as fancy or supersti-
> tion." She writes: "I have heard many stories of people
> led astray . . . by invisible power, though I myself, al-
> though born at midnight, have lived many hours of
> many years in their shades and shelters, and as the saying
> is have "never seen anything worse than myself."

She wants to hold up a "clean mirror to tradition."
   This equanimity has the effect of bringing us un-
resisting into the world of wonder reported in her
book, causing us to accept it without having to worry
the problem of our own belief. Lady Gregory is a
collector of folklore, but her attitude as the author of
Visions and Beliefs is that of an artist toward her ma-
terials: "Even when I began to gather these stories I
cared less for the evidence given in them than for the
beautiful rhythmic sentences in which they were told."
But the matter goes far beyond style. The literary world
may open beyond the edge of wonder; its boundaries
are simply what human beings may imagine. Hyacinth
Halvey is caught by some impulse and breaks away
from Cloon. We know that he needed only the right
impetus to make his break, so the extent of the moon's
power in the play is problematic, the simple talk of
Cracked Mary perhaps more decisive. Yet, at the least,

the *atmosphere* of the full moon's acting through Cracked Mary provides liberation of whatever force is necessary to bring Halvey to act upon his desires. In *Visions and Beliefs,* Lady Gregory records a number of tales of people who have gone, as the Irish say, *away* or been taken by the Sidhe, sometimes for the miraculous seven years, sometimes forever. If one finds it difficult to believe these stories, one can speculate about why they are so common. In *Poets and Dreamers,* Lady Gregory remarks that the stories told her in the Gort workhouse, with their wondrous metamorphic swans, castles, witches, and journeys to the Country of the Young, made a sharp contrast to the abject poverty of the tellers. It may be that these tales grow best among people whose lives lack variety, or perhaps among those whose imaginations have not been subjected to the restraints of more sophisticated life.

Robert Gregory remarked to his mother once that he anticipated a "return to intuition as in primitive days." His view was that reason had taken intuition's place with the Greeks but "now it has gone as far as it can go, it has ceased to interest, to satisfy." One can imagine Lady Gregory's taking this observation seriously and acting upon it by turning to plays of wonder, but at the same time keeping the wonder inside the plays, where for her it belongs, though she is always respectful of those who think otherwise.

Among people whose imaginations have not been sophisticated are children. After pressing the edges of wonder in *The Full Moon* and sending Halvey away, if only to the prosaic fair at Carrow, Lady Gregory turned her attention partly to wonder plays designed specifically for children. At the same time she became interested in severely limiting the physical scenery of these plays, perhaps partly under the influence of Yeats's similar efforts. Primarily, however, she wanted these plays easily undertaken in schools; and she wished to stimulate her childish audience to help "create" the world of *away* for themselves. So in *The Golden Apple* (published 1915), which is her longest play, there are all the trappings of a fairy-tale world—witch, giant, enchanted prince and princess, king, and court—but also a very simplified set: ". . . for the garden scene little but a well head and a little tree, and that could have been a front scene masking the King's bedchamber. The Wood of Wonders is made by the waving of boughs by the Witch and her daughter; and the Giant wants but a step-ladder and a pair of stilts." The audience provides the rest. Indeed, with children there is the problem of their providing too much. At one point a bit of playfulness reflects the comic temper of the proceedings, helps end an act, and perhaps shows that Lady Gregory did not want the little children to let their own imaginations carry them *away* to fright. The giant is made to reveal his stilts.

WIFE: You could go a short-cut through the window.
GIANT: I wonder at you! You know well to go out of the window I would have to take off my tree-legs— (*Shows stilts under his clothing.*) The people to see me that way, it is likely they would be saying me not to be a real giant!

Too much should not be made of this; it is principally a bit of fun and laughter for the audience. Beyond that, however, one may imagine that it keeps the play clearly defined for the children *as a play* or *as a flight of imagination* or *as play*. I think that this characterizes Lady Gregory's method and her own beliefs. For her the wonderful is *literary* and belongs primarily there. That is sufficient for her, and no excess flows out into belief.

As in the simple folk tale, the characters of *The Golden Apple, The Jester,* and *The Dragon* have much of the everyday world about them. Ann Saddlemyer observes that the characters of these plays are the characters of Cloon disguised. This may be insisting on too definite an equation, but the characters do have everyday traits: "the Giant . . . has a weak stomach that cannot bear the thought of blood; the Witch, harried by a selfish nagging daughter, faithfully carries out her trade . . . , the Executioner belongs to a Trade Union. . . ." In constructing her characters and her plots, Lady Gregory emphasizes a tension between hopefully imagined possibility or even the impossible and the commonplaces of human nature, reminding us that the astrologer is not infallible, the prince subject to chills like the rest of us.

The moral burden of these plays is light and somewhat ironic. It is likely to turn around upon itself in the end. In *The Jester* (1918), for example, the presiding magician, the jester himself, encourages the five little princes to change places with the five rowdy wren boys. It does not turn out to be a simple matter. The princes discover to their chagrin that the wren boys have been under the tyranny of a very unpleasant ogre, and they are soon prepared to return to their original states. Meanwhile, the wren boys, disguised as princes, find the princely life very demanding and not the mere parade of luxuries they imagined it. In the end, of course, nothing in excess. The ten go off together, the wren boys to be educated by the princes and the princes to learn about nature from the wren boys. Lady Gregory recognizes a convention of children's wonder drama, which is that the play is regarded as a step into wonder but that the audience must also be prepared to step out into the street at its end without carrying the wonder world as a burden into reality. The wonder play is an interlude.

Among the wonder plays, *The Dragon* (1919) is perhaps her greatest success. Titled *Change of Heart* in an early draft, the play makes change its theme. A young prince, dominated by his aunts, breaks away to fight a dragon; a princess who will not marry falls in love; a young king disguises himself as a cook; a dragon receives a squirrel's heart and develops a passion for nuts. In the midst of this engaging nonsense are a decrepit one-eyed wise man, an inaccurate astrologer, a fussy queen, and a gluttonous old king. The disguised hero at one point makes a remark pertinent to such plays: "Every trick is an old one, but with a change of players, a change of dress, it comes out as new as before." Lady Gregory's wonder plays for children are playful parodies of the conventions of the fairy tale.

One play evokes a special wonder and is similar to stories reported in *Visions and Beliefs*. *Aristotle's Bellows* (1921) is also most in the vein of the Cloon comedies. Set in a room in a half-ruined old castle, the play presents characters who could be living near Cloon. The central figure, Conan, is a graduate of Trinity College and is forever bemoaning the slovenliness of his family and the general decline of things since the Greeks. He would have his stepsister neater and restore his stepmother's memory, for their shortcomings annoy him sorely. He is a parody of the reformer. Quite simply, he is given the opportunity to change things through the discovery of Aristotle's marvelous bellows, capable of six magic blasts. The results are chaotic, for Conan is brought to such annoyance by his family that he impulsively expends two blasts on the domestic scene, transforming his messy sister into an outrageously compulsive housekeeper and her annoying pet pigeon into a crow. The sister forgets the bellows' power and blasts the mother with it in order to remove a crumb from her skirt. She is miraculously rendered capable of total recall and subsequently torments everyone with an unending stream of reminiscences.

The result is, of course, predictable. Conan must use his remaining blasts to return sister, mother, and bird to their former, less obnoxious states. In the end the sister applies the bellows to Conan himself and relieves him of his misanthropy. In highly satisfied good humor he lounges in a corner quoting Aristotle to the effect that there is "nothing at the end but what there used to be at the beginning."

The play embraces a theme probably representative of Lady Gregory's general view of life. Given special, unnatural powers, man does not bring about Utopia. He is shortsighted or distracted or simply too dull. There is nothing new about this; it is what T. E. Hulme labeled as classicism. Lady Gregory would have wanted to add nothing new; it jibes with her character.

But too much can be made of philosophical or moral themes in these plays. Indeed, they are most charming for their incidental comedy, which is typically of folk quality. Even kings and queens discourse on common subjects. The world of wonder blends with the everyday. In *The Dragon,* for example, the king, a compulsive eater, objects to the queen's nagging efforts to make him diet. It appears that she is what we would now call a natural food freak:

QUEEN: What's that? (*Whipping cloth from tray.*) Is it
   that you are eating again, and it is but one half-hour
   since your breakfast?
KING: Ah, that wasn't a breakfast you'd call a breakfast.
QUEEN: Very healthy food, oaten meal flummery with
   whey, and a griddle cake; dandelion tea and sorrel
   from the field.
KING: My old fathers ate their enough of wild herbs and
   the like in the early time of the world. I'm thinking
   that it is in my nature to require a good share of
   nourishment as if to make up for the hardships they
   went through.

There are numerous characters who provide opportunity for comic stage business delightful to children:
There is a doctor who must climb a ladder to examine
a giant's tongue, a dragon with a change of heart who
prefers eating a simple nut to a princess and is dis-
gusted at the very thought of blood and her hair
tickling his gullet, a giant who thinks he has swallowed
an eel—all fine opportunities for the actors.

These plays, a combination of broad humor with
wonder, make use of the world of Irish folk tale and
myth. Aristotle is the maker of the bellows because of
Aristotle's occasional appearance in tales Lady Gregory
had heard. She tells of one story reported by Douglas
Hyde in which the narrator gradually came to refer
to Aristotle, transported somehow to Ireland, as Harry.
The jester sings a song about Cuchulain, Finn, and
Osgar and reveals himself at the end as Manannan, the
Irish sea-deity, master of enchantments. The giants are
Irish Grugachs. The dragon's change of heart is taken
from an old folk tale. In all this there is Lady Gregory's
usual design. The plays children were likely to see
in Dublin were English importations. Lady Gregory's

are Irish and meant to play a modest role in the nationalist movement.

Lady Gregory's one play involving the purely supernatural in a serious vein, with the exception of the religious plays to be discussed later, is *Shanwalla* (1915). For Lennox Robinson it was "a strange, moving play out of her vein and stupidly neglected." Una Ellis-Fermor thinks it successful only as it manages a combination of mirth and pathos. Ann Saddlemyer thinks it Lady Gregory at her worst. Elizabeth Coxhead regards it as "inescapably one of her failures" and blames Lady Gregory's trying to write a play about the supernatural without any belief in its existence. The play caused much trouble in the writing. The difficulty is best revealed in a note in which Lady Gregory indicates her doubts about the use of a ghost to resolve a dramatic action. She had recorded in *Visions and Beliefs* enough instances of the unquiet dead to recognize the "consciousness of the presence of the dead" among the people of Connacht. She goes so far as to call this a "consciousness," not simply a "belief." But she proceeds to remark, ". . . I felt doubtful as to using [ghosts]; I hesitated to put them before an audience used to close reasoning and the presentation of proved facts. I feared they might be found inconclusive, trivial, meaningless." One senses here that she has projected herself, or a strong side of herself, into that audience, that she is uncomfortable with the supernatural and cannot blend her gift for low mimetic comedy with a supernatural world that is seriously perceived and not, as in the children's plays, make-believe. *Shanwalla* has its moments of comedy, but is fundamentally a melodrama complete with the tension that accompanies fear that the villain will be successful.

It includes a murder offstage, the poisoning of a race horse, a courtroom scene, and a ghost on stage.

If Lady Gregory is to be successful with the supernatural outside the children's wonder plays, it appears that it must occur in the framework of a traditional Christian orientation, with its accumulation of a moral vision attractive to her Spartan intellect. This is best illustrated by examination of her little play *The Travelling Man* and what we know of her attempted collaboration with Yeats in its construction. Much ink has been spilled speculating upon whether Yeats wrote Lady Gregory's plays or she his. The truth seems to be that on several plays, at various stages of their writing, Yeats and Lady Gregory really *collaborated*. Their talents were different, and they complemented each other. Lady Gregory had a far better sense of a play as an *action* than Yeats had or, one might say, cared to exhibit, and she had the gift of the dialect. Yeats was far more imaginatively venturesome in his themes and modes of construction, and he had a lyrical gift. Lady Gregory did not.

I examine *The Travelling Man* not in order to study their collaboration, however, even though it is most fully documented with respect to this play, but to observe how Lady Gregory handles a theme that interested them both. *The Travelling Man* was not played at the Abbey until 2 March 1910, but it was written at least eight years before, probably in the summer of 1902 when Yeats was visiting Lady Gregory at Coole. In *Our Irish Theatre* Lady Gregory wrote, *"The Travelling Man* was first my idea and then we wrote it together." Something of how they collaborated is revealed in Yeats's dedication of *Where There is Nothing*, written at the same time, to Lady Gregory:

I offer you a book which is in part your own. . . . You
said I might dictate to you, and we worked in the
mornings at Coole, and I never did anything that went
so easily and quickly; for when I hesitated you had the
right thought ready and it was almost always you who
gave the right turn to the phrase and gave it the ring
of daily life. We finished several plays, of which this is
the longest, in so few weeks that if I were to say how
few, I do not think anybody would believe me.

When Yeats had returned to London for the winter
of 1902–3, he wrote a letter to Lady Gregory on 12
December, adding the following postscript: "I will
shortly send you a new version of *The Travelling Man*
to go over for me." Then, on 16 December, he wrote
that he would like to publish the play in Volume I of
Plays for an Irish Theatre but that he could not delay
"until you come here before going to press." This
means apparently that he was waiting either for Lady
Gregory's comments or for her revisions. Lady Gregory
herself reports that she and Yeats wrote the play together; "Then Mr. Yeats wrote a variant of it as a
Pagan play, *The Black Horse,* and to this we owe the
song, 'There's many a strong farmer whose heart would
break in two.' It did not please him however, and then
I worked it out in my own way." The original draft
has not come to light, but in Yeats's papers a version
called *The Country of the Young* is clearly a draft of
the pagan version that Lady Gregory calls *The Black
Horse.* Lady Gregory worked out the play in her own
way, which involved turning it into a sort of Christian
morality play.

In her note for *The Travelling Man,* Lady Gregory
tells us that the play's origin was a story told her by
an old woman who "lived in a cabin by a bog road

on Slieve Echtge." The story appears in *Poets and Dreamers:*

> There was a poor girl walking the road one night with no place to stop; and the Saviour met her on the road, and He said: "Go up to the house you see a light in; there's a woman dead there, and they'll let you in." So she went and she found the woman laid out, and the husband and other people; but she worked harder than they all, and she stopped in the house after; and after two quarters the man married her. And one day she was sitting outside the door, picking over a bag of wheat, and the Saviour came again, with the appearance of a poor man, and He asked her for a few grains of the wheat. And she said: "Wouldn't potatoes be good enough for you?" and she called to the girl within to bring out a few potatoes. But he took nine grains of the wheat in His hand and went away; and there wasn't a grain of wheat left in the bag, but all gone. So she ran after Him then to ask Him to forgive her; and she overtook Him on the road, and she asked forgiveness. And He said: "Don't you remember the time you had no house to go to, and I met you on the road, and sent you to a house where you'd live in plenty? and now you wouldn't give Me a few grains of wheat." And she said: "But why didn't You give me a heart that would like to divide it?" That is how she came round on Him. And He said: "From this out, whenever you have plenty in your hands, divide it freely for My sake."

The Travelling Man is fairly faithful to this tale. It opens in a cottage at Samhain. A woman is preparing a cake for a feast; her child plays on the ground. He asks her what the great occasion is, and she explains that years ago she was driven from the home of her foster parents and met "The King of the World" on the road. He directed her to the house in which she found her husband-to-be. Now, her husband dead, she is waiting for the King to return, a man who carried "a green branch that never grew on a tree of this world." Then, while the mother is out of the cottage borrowing flour, a ragged traveler appears at the cottage door, carrying a branch upon which hang both apples and blossoms. The child asks where he found the branch. He replies that he found it in a garden long ago and that he comes from a country of golden mountains. The child wants to know all about the mountains and the garden, and the traveling man describes them. Then with sticks and the mother's best tableware, the child builds the garden on the floor. When it is finished the child and stranger pretend that they are riding to the new land, singing as they go. When the mother reappears, she is horrified that her child is playing with a ruffian, insists that the traveling man leave, and offers him only potatoes when he asks for food.

Just after he has left the child notices that the visitor has left his branch and runs after him with it. When the child returns the play ends with this dialogue:

CHILD: I went after him. He is gone over the river.

MOTHER: He couldn't do that. He couldn't go through the flood.

CHILD: He did go over it. He was as if walking on the water. There was a light before his feet.

MOTHER: That could not be so. What put that thought in your mind?

CHILD: I called to him to come back for the branch, and he turned where he was in the river, and he bade me to bring it back, and to show it to yourself.

MOTHER (*taking the branch*): There are fruit and flowers on it. It is a branch that is not of any earthly tree. (*Falls on her knees.*) He is gone, he is gone, and I never knew him! He was that stranger that gave me all! He is the King of the World!

Lady Gregory deletes the woman's impertinent reply to Christ that appears in the original tale, and she causes a tragic sense of moral error and loss to hang over her play's conclusion. Yeats's reworking turns the play from a Christian morality to an allegory of innocence and experience. The mother can no longer see the visitor's marvelous black horse as it flashes past. Only the young can see it.

Lady Gregory did not like Yeats's reworking and wrote to him: "I am more inclined to think the idea is the soul having once seen the Christ, the Divine Essence, must always turn back to it again." Yeats, dissatisfied too, abandoned his version. We can say, I think, that Lady Gregory's holding to the Christian theme of the original story and adding to it a more stern ending while resisting Yeats's attempts to paganize it typify her religious vision.

Two late plays, *The Story Brought by Brigit* (1924) and *Dave* (1927), reflect that vision. The first of these takes the Irish Saint Brigit, "the Mary of the Gael" as she was called, to the Holy Land to witness Christ's crucifixion. Lady Gregory had already collected stories of Brigit in her *Book of Saints and Wonders* (1906) along with legends of Columcille and Patrick. Irish tradition tells us that Mary was born in Ireland and was under Brigit's protection, and some stories say she fostered Christ. In a vision she has seen His agony and has journeyed to Jerusalem. The play has some interesting aspects, including its treatment of the politicians Marcus and Silas, and hints at parallels with Ireland: "To tell the clean truth," the Roman Marcus says, "a little Rising now and then is no harm at all. It gives us an excuse to get rid of disturbers and to bring more of our armies in. A Rising too is very apt to lead to splits, and splits are a great help when you want to keep a country down." Recent Irish history in a nutshell. But the play is unable to do much with Brigit herself, who in spite of her vision and her difficult journey has to play a spectator's and commentator's role. It is not enough to make her presence dramatically justified.

Dave, Lady Gregory's last play, is another thing entirely. It joins her religious and moral interests with a theme developed quite differently in *The Full Moon.* In the time of the famine, Dave, a seventeen-year-old youth of unknown surname and ancestry, works sullenly for Nicholas and Kate O'Cahan, under their serving man, Timothy Loughlin, who taunts him mercilessly. In the course of the play the O'Cahans set out on a journey, and the trusted Timothy immediately searches their belongings for money. When they suddenly return because of the weather, Timothy puts the blame on Dave, rushes at him, and stuns him with a violent blow. Unconscious, Dave has a vision that is partly generated by Kate's sympathetic speech to him and a report he had heard of an itinerant preacher from Connemara in the town. He undergoes a transformation. He recognizes a mission, and in its terms he is able to discover his own existence: "It would not be for honour, I go to quest or beg. I am going out as I came in, with my spade and the strength of my two hands that are all my estate. I am going in search of— to give help to— (*passes his hand over his eyes*) my people." Unlike Hyacinth Halvey's decision to escape from Cloon, his has more purpose. He has never been anybody, so he is not escaping a falsely created self.

Timothy, who has not yet been revealed as the true culprit, scoffs at him, claiming Dave will find his people in the jails or among famine-ravaged paupers of Connemara. Dave, remembering the preacher, acknowledges this, even that the most he may be able to do for some is to give them a decent burial. Kate, watching him leave, remarks: "God has surely some great hand in him. He had the look of being very glad in the mind. His head held high, and a light on his brow as bright as the bow of heaven."

A theme of this play has been names and families. O'Cahan has annoyed everyone, tracing his line back to the Battle of Clontarf and putting down his wife's family. Timothy, it turns out, descends from Danish stock, and as O'Cahan blathers on, his resentment grows. In the end Nicholas promises not to discuss the matter of names again, for identity is made, not received.

A wonder play or religious play or whatever one wishes to call it, *Dave* is simple in design and without supernatural characters or events. Dave undergoes a transformation that is natural and yet spiritual, too. It arises from within him. One senses that this mode of spiritual drama is closely akin to Lady Gregory's own vision. She has liberated Dave by allowing him to find his *work* and thus his identity. In this her last play she has turned to an idea that has governed her own experience, for she found and liberated herself in the work to which she gave herself. It was a work she regarded as the expression of devotion—to the image of an Ireland that, too, might someday find itself.

Bibliography

a. PRINCIPAL WORKS OF LADY GREGORY, ARRANGED
CHRONOLOGICALLY BY DATE OF FIRST PUBLICATION:

Arabi and His Household. London: Kegan Paul, 1882.
(ed.) *Sir William Gregory: An Autobiography.* London:
Murray, 1894.
(ed.) *Mr. Gregory's Letterbox 1813–35.* London: Murray, 1898.
(ed.) *Ideals in Ireland.* London: at the Unicorn, 1901.
Cuchulain of Muirthemne. London: Murray, 1902.
Poets and Dreamers. London: Murray, 1903.
Gods and Fighting Men. London: Murray, 1904.
A Book of Saints and Wonders. London: Murray, 1906.
The Kiltartan History Book. Dublin: Maunsel, 1909.
Seven Short Plays. Dublin: Maunsel, 1909. (Includes *The
Rising of the Moon, Spreading the News, Hyacinth
Halvey, The Gaol Gate, The Jackdaw, The Work-
house Ward, The Travelling Man.*)
The Kiltartan Wonder Book. Dublin: Maunsel, 1910.
The Kiltartan Molière. Dublin: Maunsel, 1910.
Irish Folk-History Plays (First Series). London: Putnam,
1912. (Includes *Kincora, Dervorgilla, Grania.*)
Irish Folk-History Plays (Second Series). London: Put-
nam, 1912. (Includes *The White Cockade, The Cana-
vans, The Deliverer.*)

New Comedies. London: Putnam, 1913. (Includes *The Bogie Men, The Full Moon, Coats, Damer's Gold, MacDonough's Wife.*)

Our Irish Theatre. London: Putnam, 1913.

The Kiltartan Poetry Book. London: Putnam, 1918.

Visions and Beliefs in the West of Ireland. London: Putnam, 1920.

Hugh Lane's Life and Achievement. London: Murray, 1921.

The Image and Other Plays. London: Putnam, 1922. (Includes *The Image, Hanrahan's Oath, Shanwalla, The Wrens.*)

Three Wonder Plays. London: Putnam, 1923. (Includes *The Dragon, Aristotle's Bellows, The Jester.*)

A Case for the Return of Sir Hugh Lane's Pictures to Dublin. Dublin: Talbot, 1926.

Three Last Plays. London: Putnam, 1928. (Includes *The Would-Be Gentleman, Sancho's Master, Dave.*)

My First Play: Colman and Guaire. London: Elkin Mathews and Marrot, 1930.

Coole. Dublin: Cuala, 1931.

Lady Gregory's Journals 1916–1930. Edited by Lennox Robinson. London: Putnam, 1946.

Selected Plays. Chosen and introduced by Elizabeth Coxhead. London: Putnam, 1962.

The Coole Edition of Lady Gregory's Writings. T. R. Henn and Colin Smythe, general editors. 18 vols. projected. Gerrard's Cross: Colin Smythe, 1970– . . . . .

b. BIOGRAPHIES:

Elizabeth Coxhead. *Lady Gregory: A Literary Portrait.* rev. ed. London: Secker and Warburg, 1966.

C. OTHER STUDIES:

Ernest Boyd. *The Contemporary Drama of Ireland*. Boston: Little, Brown, 1917. (Chapter on Lady Gregory)

Elizabeth Coxhead. *J. M. Synge and Lady Gregory (Writers and Their Work,* No. 149) . London: Longmans, Green, 1962.

Una Ellis-Fermor. *The Irish Dramatic Movement*. 2nd ed. London: Methuen, 1954. (Chapter on Lady Gregory)

Herbert Howarth. *The Irish Writers, 1880–1940*. New York: Hill and Wang, 1958. (Chapter on Lady Gregory)

A. E. Malone. *The Irish Drama*. London: Constable, 1929.

Lennox Robinson. *Ireland's Abbey Theatre: A History, 1899–1951*. London: Sedgwick and Jackson, 1951.

Lennox Robinson, ed. *The Irish Theatre*. London: Macmillan, 1939. (Essay on Lady Gregory by Lennox Robinson)

Ann Saddlemyer. *In Defence of Lady Gregory, Playwright*. Dublin: Dolmen, 1966.

Cornelius Weygandt. *Irish Plays and Playwrights*. Boston: Houghton Mifflin, 1913. (Chapter on Lady Gregory)